Quick Tennis

Quick Tennis

HENRY HINES
with
Carol Morgenstern

Foreword by Arthur Ashe

PHOTOGRAPHS BY
HENRY FRANK AND HERB SCULNICK

E. P. DUTTON | NEW YORK

Library of Congress Cataloging in Publication Data

Hines, Henry.
  Quick tennis.

  1. Tennis—Training. I. Morgenstern, Carol,
joint author. II. Title.
GV1002.9.T7H56 1977   796.34′2′07   77-3402

ISBN: 0-525-04275-X

Published simultaneously in Canada by Clarke, Irwin & Company
Limited, Toronto and Vancouver

10 9 8 7 6 5 4 3 2

For Karen and for my father, Henry Lloyd Hines, Jr.

H. H.

For my parents.

C. M.

Contents

Foreword

I first met Henry Hines several years ago in Tokyo, when Roscoe Tanner and I decided to attend one of his professional track meets. Roscoe and I were playing in a tennis tournament, which happened to be only 200 yards away. Being a UCLA graduate, I followed the fortunes of Southern California track stars, so the name Henry Hines was familiar to me. At the meet, Henry spotted Roscoe and me in the hallway under the stadium, came over and introduced himself, and invited us up on the track.

The way he got up there astounded us. Running alongside the track surface itself between the track and the stands was a dugout walking area, which resembled the trenches used in World Wars I and II. Standing in the trench with my chest about even with the track surface, I got a worm's-eye view of the proceedings on the track. When Henry said, "Come on up" I figured we were going to walk to our left about ten yards to the steps up to the track surface . . . wrong. Henry just took one leap and he was up there. I had never seen anybody do anything like that in my life. Needless to say, Roscoe and I walked the ten yards to the steps.

After the meet, we invited Henry over to our tournament. While watching some of us play he noticed that we were all technically competent at swinging the racquet, of course, but that we all, as he said, moved terribly. Though nobody had ever said anything like that to us before, we couldn't just dismiss it, having just seen what moving *well* looked like.

The following year, while getting ready for the 1975 season, a bunch of us Americans invited Henry down to Puerto Rico to train us. He damn near killed us for four days, but after the soreness had worn off, we were all in better shape than before and we all knew how to move more efficiently on the tennis court. 1975 just happened to be the best year I ever had . . . I wonder why.

Henry, a superb athlete, has become quite an accomplished tennis player himself; on just about any surface you can name there are very few balls he can't get to. Now Henry happens to be naturally endowed with athletic abilities we mere mortals do not have. Yet as gifted an athlete as he is, technique did play an important rôle in his rise to fame as a long-jumper. And just as Henry learned those techniques from his track coaches, we in turn have learned how to move on a tennis court from Henry Hines.

What is contained in this book is the product of three years of analyzing and playing tennis and ten years of running at a professional level. Henry's tools are a stopwatch and a towel. His students come in all shapes, sizes, colors, and ages. His subject is getting to the ball as quickly and efficiently as possible. As one of our best teaching professionals, Vic Braden, has said, "The greatest strokes in the world are no good at all if you don't get to the ball first." Henry's methods will not change your strokes or turn you into a Ken Rosewall or a Chris Evert. You might feel a little sore, a little out of breath, and, for the first few days, a little weak in the knees from his program. But if you do as he says, it will pay off: there will be times on the court when you will feel as coordinated as Olga Korbut and as quick as Ilie Nastase.

So read the book, obey the instructions carefully, and the next time you play your wife, you just might win.

ARTHUR R. ASHE, JR.

Quick Tennis

1⚾ Tennis Is a Running Game

In April, 1973, I was in Tokyo with the International Track Association for a meet. I had joined the pro track tour seven months earlier and was long-jumping my way around the world while I wondered what I was going to do with the rest of my life. I read in the newspaper that a tennis tournament was also being held there, and that Arthur Ashe was playing in it. Though I had never met Ashe, I admired him a great deal: he was the only black guy playing professional tennis. As he has just told you, he and Roscoe Tanner came to my meet (getting there the hard way), and I went to their matches. We became friends, and back in the States, I began to follow their careers. When either of them played in a tournament in L.A., I'd be there. When they were on TV, I'd watch them. Soon I began playing tennis myself. Almost from my first day on a tennis court, I found that I could get to the ball more quickly than they could. Roscoe, when he saw me move on the court, said, "Henry, a lot of us pros are sure glad you took up track instead of tennis." Initially, I figured the reason I was so quick was that I was a trained track man. But then I saw that track friends of mine who could run the 100 much faster than I could weren't getting to those balls, either. I realized that track speed—velocity—isn't the important thing

1

on the tennis court; quickness—the ability to react rapidly—and technique are.

It was clear that Ashe and Tanner, for all their experience and power, lacked mobility. When I watched them I'd ask myself, "Why did he have to lunge for that drop shot? Why did he miss that wide forehand? Why did he fail to change direction in time?" I started taking notes: *"When the ball's hit to him he pops up before he starts running. He's running on his heels."* I started thinking about *why* the players were moving incorrectly and figured out that they were probably popping up when they started running because they were standing up too straight to begin with. I tried it myself and saw that my lower position allowed me to stop, go, move, and be generally more agile. I concluded that if they wanted to be quicker, to stop running on their heels and popping up, they would have to play lower.

I started watching other players, studying how they got to all kinds of shots, noting what they did after they hit their shots, analyzing everything they did and didn't do in covering the court. They *all* did things that didn't look right to me, major and minor things that seemed to keep them from getting into the right position at the right time to do the right thing. I had started playing five, six hours a day, and I was trying out everything that I observed. By combining what I knew about efficient motion from track with studying and playing tennis, I began to come up with some basic principles for efficient motion on the tennis court. For example, I saw that the easiest balls to hit were the ones that came right to me. When I ran through my shots, I didn't have nearly the control that I had when I was stationary. Therefore, I reasoned, if you can hustle and set up for your shot early instead of just jogging after the ball and running through it, you can hit the ball *as if* it had come right to you in the first place.

Though track—the long jump—was the sport to which I became totally dedicated late in high school and throughout college, working to achieve mastery over one sport or another seems to have always been a major theme in my life. First it was Little League, then football, then judo—I was a brown belt when I was twelve years old. I had a long romance with the rodeo, riding broncos and Brahma bulls. I also rode in *gymkhanas* —agility meets for horses. I even spent a year training horses for them.

But when I discovered track, everything else took a back seat—other sports, school, girls, even my horse. My sister Pam, who was a great sprinter, beat me in a race while the entire school looked on, and I was *mad*. I threw myself into track with a vengeance, becoming good enough to compete in a number of events: the 100, the quarter-mile, the 440 relay, the javelin, the high hurdles, the triple jump, and the long jump. By my senior year of high school, it was clear that the event with my name on it was the long jump. For the next five years, just about the only thing that mattered to me was being the best long jumper I could possibly be. Winning gold medals was what life seemed for. I was number one in the world in 1972, before the Olympics, when I injured my back in a pretrial meet. The Olympics, somehow, took place without me.

Track had made me very detail-oriented. When I was long jumping in college I used to study films of all the great long jumpers: Bob Beamon, Ralph Boston, Gail Hopkins, Arnie Robinson. I'd run the films back and forth, back and forth, for hours at a time, analyzing every movement of every muscle from the moment those guys started down the runway to the moment they landed in the pit: where their eyes were looking; the position of their heads, hips, backs, stomachs, chests, arms, hands, legs, and feet throughout the run, the gather, the take-off, the flight, and the landing. I got so I knew everyone's jump perfectly. I would try out everything I observed and then incorporate into my jump whatever made it stronger.

As a result, I felt right at home studying tennis players' movements on the court. For instance, I'd notice which foot a player would start with when a cross-court ball was hit to him. I saw that when he anticipated it correctly, he usually led with what I thought was the correct leg; when he anticipated incorrectly, he often led with the wrong leg. I figured out that if the players were committing their balance the wrong way, they often had to compensate by doing the next thing wrong, too. I experimented, and concluded that keeping your balance squared away—uncommitted—will always permit you to pivot correctly from the very beginning.

At one point, I asked Arthur and Roscoe if they ever stretched and loosened up before they played. They answered, "Not really. We just hit to warm up." They were especially impressed by my looseness and flexibility, and figured that that was probably one of the main reasons I was so well balanced when I moved. Agreeing that stretching out first would probably help them feel better, get more limber, and enable them to do more with their bodies, they asked me for some exercises. Since each sport uses different sets of muscles, each requires a warm-up specifically for that sport; even in track and field, hurdlers stretch out differently from long jumpers, sprinters differently from distance runners. I sat down and thought: ". . . *playing lower . . . moving . . . using arms . . .*" and came up with a series of stretching exercises to loosen all the muscles tennis players use on the court. I also put together a workout program to strengthen the muscles that they would particularly need to maintain their new, lower positions. Since the body doesn't work any harder than you make it work, these muscles were undeveloped because the players had been playing tall so long. I then designed a set of running drills that would help them develop more quickness, agility, balance, and control. After sifting through hundreds of ideas, inventing, adapting, changing, eliminating—the test being what *worked*—I eventually evolved a program specifically geared to improving mobility on the tennis court.

The first player I actually worked with was Roscoe Tanner. We went over to a park near my home and worked out on the grass. The session was a great success. By the end of that first day, Roscoe had a good idea of what his weak spots were and what he could do to strengthen them. For example, we did the Eight-Second Drill, a fast foot exercise that showed him both how quickly he could move his feet and also how weak his leg muscles were, which is something that drill brings out—as you'll soon see. Tanner concluded that if he wanted to be quicker he'd have to strengthen his legs. He did the Balance and Motion Triangle, a running drill that challenges and improves balance, several times under the stopwatch, which showed him what it would take to control his balance as he changed direction quickly. We got into toe leads, cross-court pivots, arm drives. I timed him doing things right and doing them wrong, which helped bring my ideas home. Soon he started practicing and applying the techniques we worked on that day and subsequently, and before long his friends, who are, after all, his opponents on the court, were taking notice.

I began filming him and Ashe and going over their motion problems with them. Then in January, 1975, I went down to Puerto Rico, where eight of the top pros had put together a kind of training camp for themselves before the season started. We went through my entire program, and, as Arthur has told you, those guys got a real workout. I started working regularly with tennis pros: drilling, filming, teaching them how to get off the mark more quickly, how to have better balance, how to run to the ball more efficiently. No one had ever really helped them with movement before, and there was a great need for it. As tennis has become more popular, more and more major tournaments are being played on slower surfaces to keep the game spectator-oriented—tennis fans would rather see a match where five or six strokes are being hit per point than just a big serve and a winning volley, where the point is over in a matter of seconds. Even the big servers are being forced to learn to cover the court well because on clay, their big serves come right back at them. On top of this, now that the prize money is so high in professional tennis, the level of competitiveness has risen to new heights, and the players are starting to play aggressive, quick tennis even on clay. Clay is a tough surface to move well on, and any player who really doesn't know his way around on it now is going to get left behind. It's not enough anymore just to have good strokes; these days it's the players who are also quick on their feet who win tournaments.

The clinics for amateurs got started after an article about me in *World Tennis* included my address. Thousands of people wrote me with questions about warm-ups, workouts, drills, and techniques. I started with a few small groups; they went well, and now in addition to coaching professionals, I run two-day clinics for twenty to thirty amateurs at a time. Young players, old players, beginners and advanced—there's usually the whole gamut in each clinic and everyone learns a lot and has a good time. My amateur clinics are exactly the same as my workouts with the pros, only a little less strenuous. And this book explains the same principles that are actually used in my workouts and clinics, except that I'm not there in person to clock you and carry on like a drill sergeant or a mother hen.

Have you ever wondered why, no matter how hard you try, you can never quite manage to reach a certain opponent's cross-court forehand? By the time you get over there, flailing desperately with your racket, the damn ball has just gotten behind you. Or why, when you're at the net and your opponent makes an average shot, it ends up passing you, and you've been working on your volley for months? Do you ever find yourself just standing up at the net with your feet planted, watching the ball bounce, when your opponent has sailed a lob over your head, half because you don't think you're fast enough to chase it back and half because you have no idea how to get there? Have you ever wondered how the guy on the next court can retrieve practically any ball his opponent hits, no matter where it lands, and how he always manages to get back into position for the next one?

This is a tennis instruction book that won't tell you a single thing about how to hold your racket, or how to stroke the ball. It also won't tell you anything about strategy, or the winning attitude, or what you should do if your doubles partner can't volley but insists on poaching at the net. What this book *will* teach you is *how to cover the court,* how to get to the ball so you can start reaching all those shots that seem to land just beyond your range, the ones you could control if only you could get started more quickly and knew how to run them down.

The difference between a well-hit and a mis-hit shot is often no more than a fraction of a second, gained or lost because of movement techniques. I've become more and more convinced that very few tennis players—professionals or amateurs—know how to move quickly and efficiently on the tennis court. Many players who have classic Pancho Gonzales strokes can't get themselves to the ball in time to *use* those strokes. Much of the time they're completely out of position. They look beautiful, those strokes, but tennis is a competitive sport, not a beauty contest, and if you can't reach the ball in time to set up properly, the best strokes in the world won't do you a bit of good.

So I teach the bottom half of the game: the footwork. I'll teach you how to get from point A to point B on a tennis court with finesse, control, and balance. I'll also help you get your feet and your body out of the way of your strokes, so you can start using them to your best advantage. The overall goal of this program is to help you be the best athlete and tennis player you can possibly be by working on six fundamental qualities:

1. *Flexibility.* You can't run well if you're tight. One of the things that has helped Roscoe Tanner—who used to be known not only for his lightning-fast serve but also for his awful, lumbering slowness on the court—become so much quicker in the past few years is that he started to work on loosening up his stiff muscles. His opponents still can't believe it when they see him streak across the court and get to the ball. He's even playing a different game now: percentage tennis. Now that he can move, he has the confidence to wait for the right shot and knows he can stay out on the court as long as necessary.

In order to be a quicker, more athletic tennis player, you're going to have to be flexible. You'll be putting demands on your body that it's probably never gone through before. If your muscles, ligaments, and tendons aren't limber and stretched out, you won't be able to make them do what you want and you could hurt yourself trying.

2. *Agility.* There are some drills in this book that will show you just how agile you are or aren't. Doing them will make you more agile—maybe not quite catlike, but certainly better able to react on the court in a manner that gets the job done.

3. *Balance.* A lot of players have problems with balance—they overcommit their weight in one direction or another and often get caught wrong-footed. There is a drill in this book that can improve your balance to the extent that you'll be able to make 360-degree turns at full speed with no problems. Since this is a much more radical directional change than you will ever need to make on a tennis court, if you can do this drill right you should have very little trouble with lesser changes of direction— say, getting to the side quickly for a ball that's on its way down the line.

4. *Footwork.* Most players don't know what to do with their feet when they go for the ball—how to get started, which leg to lead with, which part of the foot to run on, what length of stride to take. I see people all the time landing on their heels and off-balance, or getting to the ball on the wrong foot and then having to lunge wildly just to get their rackets on it.

Bad footwork, not bad strokes, is probably the major cause of errors on the tennis court. People try to hit their strokes with their feet and bodies out of position, then they miss their shots and blame it on their forehand or their backhand, when the problem is generally on the bottom. Ashe and Pasarell estimate that getting in position to hit the ball is seventy percent of the game. All players are capable of moving much more effectively, if they work on it and have some faith in themselves.

There are a few gifted players—very few—who move well naturally, without thinking about it much; but we can't all be Nastases and Goolagongs. Unfortunately, most teaching pros don't teach footwork at all. Pros teach strokes, not running; most of them don't know enough about running to help their students become quicker on the court. Over and over I talk to people in my clinics who complain that their teaching pros never go any farther about footwork than to say "Step into the ball." Nothing about how to get going quickly, how to stop and set up, how to move across the court, how to recover.

Most players who have moved past the beginning stages of the game can handle *inner balls*—balls that come right to them or near them, within what I call their *comfort range*—without much trouble. The problems begin with *outer balls,* ones they have to run down. That's when they start lunging and dragging and lurching all over the court. This book will introduce you to the basic techniques of moving, both for the outer balls, the ones you probably often end up running through now, and the inner balls, which are your bread-and-butter shots.

5. *Quickness.* The quick players, the ones who move well, are the ones who win matches against their peers and can often stay on the court with players who have superior strokes. In professional tennis, as the players themselves will tell you, very few players who are slow are winning singles matches. By *quick,* as I said earlier, I don't mean *fast*; there's a big difference. I know a couple of sprinters who can run the hundred in 9.1 but often can't get to a drop shot, because they're just not quick enough. Quickness is a matter of taking off for short bursts of speed, which is what you need to reach those drop shots, lobs, and other balls beyond your range. It's actually the first stage you run through on the way to reaching your maximum speed, but in tennis you don't need to go past that first stage. A large part of quickness is reflexes. I've got a couple of drills to help you sharpen yours.

6. *Conditioning.* Most tennis players are simply not in good shape. Many people's bodies quit on them after only one or two sets. A lot of players I've worked with believe they're in shape until we start working out, when they begin huffing and puffing and groaning and complaining and finding out what it means to *really* be in shape. Especially for many of the women in my clinics, it's been an absolute revelation that to be quick you need to be strong, which means firming up the body. Conditioning—more strength and better endurance—is one of the end results of the program, a very important one because it's what will allow you to go three fast sets and still maintain a high degree of effectiveness on the court. A lot of matches are won and lost just at that point when one player begins to dog it.

This book can help you improve your game in these six areas. It can push your overall game up a notch or two and give you a big advantage over the guy or gal whose strokes are as good as yours. If you're like most people, feeling satisfied when you come off the court depends at least as much on victory over yourself as on victory over your opponent. Knowing how to cover the court effectively and knowing you have the strength and stamina to play your best until the match is over will not only make you a more confident, competent tennis player; it will also make playing tennis a richer experience for you. A friend of mine once summed it up beautifully when we were discussing the joys of tennis: "Owning your own body on the court will help put tennis on the precious list of things you do well."

2 ⓪ Warming Up

Does it sometimes take a whole set before you really get into the match? If so, I think I know what your problem is. Tennis players hardly ever warm up properly before they play, not only amateurs but top professionals as well. To most players, "warming up" means rallying for ten minutes, if that long; practicing a couple of volleys, serves, and overheads; and then somebody says, "You ready? Up or down?" Typically, these players then get locked into a kind of uncontrolled, unathletic, unwilling game in which their minds are urging, "Let's go! Let's go!" but their bodies are protesting, "Hey, hold on. Let's just wait a minute here until we get ready." Sometimes unprepared players wind up pulling a hamstring, a groin muscle, or a back muscle, and have to spend the rest of the season watching other people play tennis. Most of the time they get away without hurting themselves, just losing a lot of points unnecessarily because their bodies are still cold. There are many more muscles involved in playing tennis besides the ones in your arms and back, which are the only ones you stretch out if you warm up by just hitting.

A series of good stretching and loosening-up exercises will do three very important things for you: get you ready to come out smoking on the first point, reduce your chances of injuring yourself, and, if you do them more or less regularly, make you more flexible—in other words, improve the elasticity of your muscles, tendons, and ligaments—which is very important if you want to be really mobile on the tennis court. Tanner, for instance, has noticed that he is able to change direction much more quickly since he's been doing these exercises. If you're tight, you'll move awkwardly. If you're loose and stretched out, you'll move with more fluidity.

Very few people are really flexible without working at it, and anyone who does work at it can be more flexible, whatever his age or the current condition of his body. While flexibility decreases with age, I've found that even most of the guys and gals on the college tennis teams I've worked with have been extremely tight. John Andrews, a young pro I work with, notices that he particularly needs to stretch out when he's in training, because that's when his muscles really tighten up. In other words, stretching exercises are for everybody—kids, juniors, seniors, professional athletes, and everyone in between.

Warming up is a transition from rest to activity; it's natural, it's necessary, and it feels good. When a cat gets up from a nap, it doesn't take a single step until it's stretched the whole length of its body, front to back. You probably do the same thing to some extent when you wake up in the morning. But tennis players were never really taught to stretch their bodies systematically, even though before such a demanding sport as tennis it's close to essential. Until recently, the only players who ever bothered with it were the ones who were nursing injuries, like Bob Lutz and Stan Smith.

Muscles work by contracting and relaxing. When you start moving a muscle that has been inactive, its first few contractions and relaxations are going to be weak and irregular—that's why those first few shots you hit are usually so uncoordinated. Besides literally raising the temperature of your muscles and increasing their blood and oxygen supplies, warming up also increases the strength of their contractions and relaxations. That's how it can help you be more coordinated when you start playing.

A sudden, unprepared, strenuous activity like running can extend a cold muscle too quickly and increase the chances of injuring it. It's not all that different from what happens to taffy if you try to stretch it too fast. Now that they're in their thirties, a lot of the pros do these stretches every day, even on days they're not playing, because otherwise their muscles would tighten up and could get them into trouble. In fact, one man who took my clinic, who had a bad knee from an old football injury, got into the habit of exercising regularly before playing tennis and found that his knee didn't give him any more problems when he played. Just once he failed to warm up, and his knee started to bother him again. Now he's a believer. While I can't promise you that kind of near-miracle, I do know that a warmed-up, stretched muscle or ligament is much less injury-prone than a cold, tight, sleepy one.

Incidentally, most people who do exercise before they play only bother with it on cold days, which is a big mistake and the reason more athletes pull muscles in hot weather than in cold. The temperature outside has nothing to do with your internal temperature, which is what we're concerned about. Getting warmed up may be easier when it's ninety-four degrees outside, but it's just as important as when it's forty-nine.

I guarantee it: fifteen minutes of stretching exercises before you start hitting will do you and your game a lot more good than fifteen minutes of just rallying. These days, more and more of the guys and gals on the pro tour are rallying before matches simply to groove their strokes a bit—they've already done their warming up off the court. A lot of them used to be slow getting started; they felt they needed three or four games just to loosen up. Now they're ready to get the edge on an opponent right at the beginning of the match. Besides, now that there are tournaments practically every week of the year, players are getting hurt more—tennis elbows, pulled muscles, sprains. Warming up provides them with some insurance against injuries. So even if you're skeptical, give it a try. Think of it this way: if you've rented a court for an hour, why waste part of your court time warming up? I know at least one woman who does the exercises at home just before she leaves to play tennis. Another clinic graduate, a fifteen-year-old girl who plays number one on her high-school team, taught her teammates the warm-ups, and now the whole team does them religiously before practice, and of course before matches.

Recently I was talking to the man with the old football injury, who told me, "A couple of the guys I play with laugh at me for doing warm-up exercises. Let them laugh. I just won the C tournament at my club for the first time."

You'll probably recognize some of these exercises. I chose them because together they get the job done of warming up and stretching all the muscles, tendons, and ligaments you use in tennis. Do them in the correct sequence, because that way in the earlier exercises you warm up the muscles you stretch in the later ones. Breathe regularly, and go at your own pace. Don't try to force your body into shape; coax it; and don't feel discouraged if you can't assume all the correct positions at first—neither could most of the professionals I've taught them to. You'll get more flexible as you keep it up.

Like everything else, you get out of exercise what you put into it. The warm-ups will do you a lot more good if you do them with *full range of motion,* which means stretching until you've reached the maximum extension allowed by a particular muscle. Stretching slowly and holding the stretch for a few seconds is both safer and more effective than bobbing up and down. You're just asking for trouble if you try to do too much too fast. Concentrate more on quality than on quantity. I've indicated the number of times you should repeat each exercise, but just use my numbers as guidelines; only you know when you feel loose enough. At first, you may find these exercises taking more time than you'd like—half an hour or so—but as you get stronger and more accustomed to doing them, you'll find your time coming down to twelve or fifteen minutes.

Your muscles draw up while you're playing, so between points, between games, whenever there's a break in the action, do some more stretches. Whatever feels tight, stretch it back out again.

After you've played two or three sets, you probably feel like taking a break for half an hour or so. Before getting back on the court, loosen up again. This will help you avoid that sluggish feeling players often have when they resume play after a long break.

There are times, I realize, when you don't have fifteen minutes to warm up off the court. You've reserved a court from 2 to 3 and it's 1:55. In that case, just concentrate on your arms and legs: do the arm rotations and the Hurdlers' Exercise. Don't do too much stretching if you haven't broken a sweat first, and play easy at the beginning: try not to stop too short and don't give your strokes or your practice serves everything you've got. Then, between points, between games, whenever you have a minute, work in a few more stretches. In other words, when you don't have time beforehand, warm up during the match, as early into it as possible. Realize, however, that the more important the match is to you, the more you have to come in with both sides blazing!

1. *Breaking a Sweat.* The first thing we do is jog around a little bit, or run in place if space is limited, taking short, slow, relaxed strides. There's no set number of laps; just run until you break a little sweat under your arms. One woman I know runs around the court four times. Jogging will not get you in top shape and should not make you tired. It's just to get your heart pumping and your circulation going—like warming up a cold engine.

2. *Neck Rotations.* We start at the neck, go all the way down to the feet, and loosen up everything in between. A lot of muscles connected to your arms, back, and legs start in your neck, which is really the top of your spine and a tension center for many people. This makes it a good place to start loosening up your whole body.

Stand with your feet about shoulder-width apart, put your arms by your sides, and relax. Now rotate your head slowly all the way around, with full range of motion. The cracking you may hear is just like what happens when you crack your knuckles and is nothing to worry about. While your head is down, press your chin into your chest a bit to pull up your back muscles. Usually five times around to the left, then five times to the right will get the job done, but if you're especially tense, or just waiting around, do what Bob Lutz calls "360 on the neck" until you feel good.

(*Above, Left*) Neck rotations. Rotate your head slowly all the way around. (*Above, Right*) Shoulder Rotations. Make full circles with your shoulders. (*Below, Left*) Arm Rotations. Let your arms circle freely; your fingertips should tingle. (*Below, Right*) Trunk rotations. Just swing from side to side with full range of motion.

3. *Shoulder Rotations.*   These loosen your back and shoulders, usually a very tight, weak area. In the same stance you use for neck rotations, rotate your shoulders in full circles. Raise them as high as you can, push them all the way back, then down as low as you can, and around in front as far forward as you can. Up, back, around and down, vigorously. Make the motion round, not square. Don't thrust your head forward, and keep your neck relaxed. If you find yourself getting a little tired from these, it's because your deltoid muscles are weak, and if you're weak in there you can imagine what's hampering some of your shots—particularly your overheads and serves. I get a bit tired from these myself, and so do a lot of the players I've worked with, so don't feel as though you're hopelessly out of shape. Do twenty forward, twenty backward, quickly—approximately twenty per ten seconds.

4. *Arm Rotations.*   For your shoulders, arms, and back. With your feet shoulder-width apart, extend your arms directly out in front of you. Swing them around vigorously in wide circles, up, back, and around. Don't "muscle" your arms; let them swing freely, because muscling them around would just tense them up, and what we're striving for is freedom of motion. If you're doing it correctly, this exercise should make your fingertips tingle because blood is being pumped into them. Do twenty-five forward, twenty-five backward.

5. *Trunk Rotations.*   To loosen your back and hip area. Stand with your feet shoulder-width apart and push your hips forward slightly. Just swing around from side to side, letting your arms float freely. Don't stop abruptly; ease into the stops. When you twist to the right, let your left foot rise up onto your toes, and vice versa, which will give you more freedom of motion. Do ten in each direction.

6. *Hamstring Stretch.*   This is designed to stretch the muscle behind your thigh, the hamstring. Hamstring pulls are a common sports injury.

(*Left*) Hamstring Stretch A. Hold your maximum position; don't bob up and down.

(*Below*) Hamstring Stretch B. Try to make an ever-widening arc.

(*Bottom*) Hamstring Stretch C. Reach way around from side to side in slow semicircles.

a. With your feet a little closer together than shoulder-width apart, extend your arms down as far as your legs will let you go without either bending your knees or straining yourself—just a bit past where it's comfortable but not to the point of pain. Think you're not reaching down as far as you should be at first? Well, Ray Moore, Charles Pasarell, Roscoe Tanner, and a few of the other guys and gals on the pro tour probably didn't get as low as you are now. One player could barely get to his knees. With regular practice, you'll be getting your hands to the ground. Bend down and hold your position for a count of six, then come up. Stay relaxed. Try to go down perhaps a quarter-inch or half-inch farther each time, or if you loafed last time try to go down a whole inch farther. Make a little increment of progress each time, not more than you can take, and don't bob up and down. If you try to do too much too fast you're going to hurt yourself; we're trying to get you quicker on the court, not laid up in bed. Four of these should get you limber enough for the next phase.

b. Spread your feet about one foot wider. Keep your knees straight, bend down, and reach out with both hands as far as you can in front of you, with your fingers touching the ground. Now swing your body all the way around to the left, keeping your fingers on the ground, then way around as far as you can reach out in front, and all the way around to the right. Draw an imaginary line between your heels, extend it out a few feet, and try to go from that point on one side to that point on the other side, reaching forward a little farther each time, making an ever-widening, semicircular arc. Make a mark in front of yourself so you can try to go a little bit past it. A quarter of an inch here, a quarter of an inch there, pay big dividends later on the court. I'm not trying to turn you into Kathy Rigby or Nadia Comaneci, just helping you get limber enough to do what you have to do on the court. Pay the price now and get the benefits later on.

c. Now spread your legs as far out to the sides as you can possibly stand it. Just take them and jam them out there. Do the same thing in this position: reach way around from side to side

(*Left*) Groin Stretch. Push outward with your elbows.

(*Below*) Bridge. Try to reach a little farther out and around each time.

(*Bottom*) Hurdler's Exercise. Stretch over your straight leg without bobbing.

in slow semicircles. Yes, that's where the pain is, that's where it feels uncomfortable, uncoordinated, and clumsy, but that's where the benefit is, that's where the progress is made, going a little farther than you'd like. Just do a couple here and then come back out of this position because you're putting a lot of strain on yourself right now and all we're trying to do is to begin to loosen you up a bit.

7. *Groin Stretch.* Probably the most common leg-muscle injury is not to the hamstring or the quadriceps but to the groin muscle. People slip, stretch their legs out too far, and then pull it. This area is subject to enormous stress in running and is also probably the most neglected area when it comes to stretching. You don't want a pulled groin muscle, and neither does your husband, wife, boyfriend, or girl friend.

With your feet about a foot or so more than shoulder-width apart, squat down between your legs and tuck your rear end in. You should be flat-footed. Fit your elbows in the inside bend of your knees and push outward with your elbows. Hold for six seconds. Do three times.

8. *Bridge.* Staying in the squatting position, shift your weight all the way to the left, and then extend your right leg. Your legs should form a ninety-degree angle. You might find this tough to do at first; you may be able to balance better if you put the heel of your foot directly under you. Now extend your arms out in front, fingers lightly touching the ground, and rotate your body in a semicircular arc, putting your chest over your straight leg, then over your bent leg. Each time try to reach a little farther out and around. Work on maintaining your balance; it will improve with practice. Do four each way. Then shift your weight across, staying as low as possible, and reverse legs, doing the exercise with your left leg extended. Work on each leg two times.

9. *Hurdler's Exercise.* If you only have time to do one exercise, this should be the one. It's just about the best stretching exercise ever devised by man for your legs because it works on your whole leg—top, bottom, front, and back.

(*Top*) When you can "eat the grass," you're really loose. (*Center*) Try to put your chest on your bent leg, but don't expect to come close at first. (*Bottom*) Lie straight back to stretch your quadriceps.

Use a towel or a mat if you're warming up on a hard surface. Sit down. Extend your right leg and bend your left leg beside you, forming a ninety-degree angle with your legs. Reach down over your right leg, stretching over as far as possible, and hold at maximum stretch without bobbing for a count of six. Then come up. Do this four times, trying to stretch a little farther each time. A fraction of an inch is good progress. Eventually you'll be able to "kiss your knee," believe it or not. If you can already do that, reach out a little farther with your hands and try putting your head to the ground along the inside of your knee. Between each repetition, you may want to bounce your leg up and down a few times to relax it, but remember not to bounce your body over your leg while you're stretching it.

Now extend your arms straight out between your legs and stretch down as far between them as you possibly can. Hold for six counts, and come up. Do this four times. The idea is to make progress toward putting your face on the ground. You'll probably only get down three or four inches in that direction at first. When you can put your face on the ground and "eat the grass" under you, then you are *loose*. Believe me, when I started out with Tanner, Gorman, Moore, Ashe, Smith, Andrews, and the rest of those guys, they were the absolute worst at this. Some of them had never stretched a leg muscle before in their lives. Guys who couldn't move two inches toward the ground at first are all "eating the grass" now, not because they're professional tennis players but because they stretch out regularly now. So don't be disappointed by your lack of progress early on, because it never happens immediately. I can still remember the feeling of achievement I had when I finally got down there.

Now stretch over the bent left leg, trying to put your chest on your left leg. Absolutely no one does well in this position at first, because the ligament involved here is a very short one. Go slowly, holding for six counts. Do this four times.

Now, keeping your legs right where they are and maintaining the ninety-degree angle between them, lie straight back. You may have to raise your bent knee to get your back down, but try to lower the knee again. You're stretching your quadriceps, the muscle on top of the thigh. This is a very important stretch because it's the only one in the series for the quad. Stay down for a count of six.

Now sit up, reverse legs, and repeat the entire exercise, stretching over the top of the left leg, into the middle, and over the bent right leg, four times each, holding for six counts. Then lie straight back in line with your bent leg for six counts. Do this exercise slowly, and try to make a little progress with each repetition.

10. *Jump-ups.* Finally, an easy one: do twenty-five, jumping up as high as you can by springing off your toes.

3 ⊗ Ready for Anything

Now that you've loosened up all your tennis muscles, you're ready to get ready. The correct ready position is as basic to moving efficiently on the tennis court as the proper grip is to hitting a good forehand. Getting ready properly will help you to concentrate on the game from the body upward: you will find that in readying yourself on the court, you will also be readying yourself in your mind; your mind and your body will be on their way to working in conjunction with each other.

Get down in what you think is a good ready position, the one your local pro or whoever taught you this game showed you. Take a look at yourself. How far apart are your feet? Where are your toes pointed? Where is your weight centered—in front of you, behind you, directly over your feet? Are you low to the ground or high?

The quickest, most prepared, and most solid way to wait for the ball is to get your weight *low* and *forward*. Here's why: your center of gravity, located in the vicinity of your navel, is the point around which your weight is equally distributed. The lower your center of gravity and the wider your base of support—your feet—the more stable you'll be. Your weight should be forward because forward is where you're going; if your center of gravity isn't out in front, you might as well be glued to the ground.

A good ready position should make you feel both comfortable and aggressive. First of all, stand with your feet about shoulder-width apart, or maybe even a little wider, your weight equally balanced on both feet. Bend down and put your hands on your knees as if you were getting ready to look through a keyhole. Make sure your knees are comfortably flexed, not locked behind you. Right now you're in a fairly good ready position, but not the best, because your weight and your balance are not yet working for you at maximum efficiency. If you shift your weight forward just a hair, you'll be in perfect position. Shift forward enough so that there's a definite weight transfer off your heels and onto the balls of your feet, but don't lift your heels four inches off the ground—no more than an inch at the most. Maintain an *equal profile,* by which I mean keep your whole body in line both vertically and horizontally. Keep your head up, and don't tilt it to

Feet shoulder-width apart, knees flexed, put your hands on your knees . . . then shift your weight forward slightly.

either side, or raise one shoulder, or one hip. Like an airplane flying, slight resistance and superfluous movements will affect your body's motion a great deal. The idea is to be ready to go in any direction in a flash, and if you've already committed even a small portion of your weight in one direction or another before you know where you want to go, you're starting off with one strike against you. In fact you should be centered, or squared away, all the time—in ready position, while you're moving, when you stop.—This will help you avoid getting wrong-footed by making it a lot easier for you to stay balanced and to go back to where you came from if necessary.

Now pick up your racket and feel the position that you're in by shifting your weight back and forth from your heels onto the balls of your feet, like a tiger that's crouching low, getting ready to spring. This is the position that will allow you to move left, move right, move forward, get back, jump up in the air, and do anything you have to do on the court very quickly.

Perfect ready position: alert, weight forward, equal profile, ready to spring.

I can describe the correct position, but *you* have to feel it. The most important thing is to get your weight forward by getting off your heels; but you don't have to be flat-footed or stiff-kneed to be unready. You can be on the balls of your feet and *still* be wrong, with your weight slumped back in your seat—just "posing." Or you can be *too* far forward, which is just as bad as being too far backward: you'd be off-balance, and besides, you can't go back quickly if your weight is *way* out in front. You also don't want to be so low that you'd cramp your shots, or so wide that you can't move. You know you're in good ready position if you feel you can take off like a shot in any direction.

This is the position you should immediately and automatically *recover* into after every shot you hit until you've won the point (might as well think positively) and it's time to collect the balls. Hit, get back in ready position, and then return into the court by skipping sideways—shuffling—in your ready/recovery position, staying on your toes and squared away. Because you're not committing your balance, as you are when you run, shuffling is the best way to regain ground after you've hit and you're waiting for your opponent's next shot.

Particularly when the game is getting aggressive, you've got to maintain this *aggressive profile,* low and forward, which will allow you the maximum opportunity to shift, run, hit, dart, stop, go, jump—in short, be completely mobile. Anything less than the position you're in right now is not desirable when you're trying to control the inner balls—the ones within your range—and get to those outer balls—the ones you have to run for—that are giving you problems. If you're having difficulty reaching outer balls, you can be pretty sure that one root of the problem is the position that you left from, which probably wasn't aggressive enough to let you get started quickly.

As soon as you start playing in this good ready position, you will begin to realize the extent to which tennis is a game of position and movement as well as a game of strokes. It's absolutely the best all-purpose position in which to wait for any ball, including a serve. It will enable you to keep your balance if you have to return a hard-hit serve, or to get a quick, controlled start if

Incorrect ready position: flat-footed and weight committed to one side.

you have to return a serve that spins away. It's the position that will allow you to get to the net quickly and to cover it effectively once you're up there. Wherever you are on the court, if you're not hitting or running or setting up for your shot, you should be in this ready/recovery/return-of-serve position, with certain variations for different situations, which I'll get into next. If your back, stomach, and leg muscles aren't in shape, you're going to get too fatigued to maintain this position throughout a long match; but if you do the workouts in Chapter 9, you should have no problems with it at all.

BASELINE AND NET PROFILE

There are basically three types of tennis players: the back-court player, the serve-and-volleyer, and the all-court player, who is at home back on the baseline or up at the net, depending on the situation—his opponent's game, the court surface, the score, and so forth. Of course, whether you prefer to take the offensive by attacking the net or to stand on the baseline and attempt to out-steady your opponent is a matter of personality as well as of your particular talents and skills on the court. But whatever your style of game, you have to gear it to the aggressiveness of the match you're playing—the more aggressive the tennis, the quicker and more ready you have to be.

If you're playing on the baseline and everything's going your way—your opponent is on the defensive, running all over the court, hitting right to you—then you can relax a little, recovering a bit taller, say, than into your standard ready position. You should always maintain a forward profile, but you can come up slightly from the waist. However, be prepared, because anything might happen. All of a sudden, your opponent might get a chance to knock the cover off the ball, or to surprise you with a little dink shot. You'd never make it if you were standing pat, on your heels. Or he could be hitting you a series of easy cross-court shots and then hit two in a row to the same side, catching you going the wrong way. It's one of the oldest and most effective patterns in tennis. Don't let yourself be lulled into complacency by a long baseline rally. You've got to be ready for anything.

On the other hand, if *you're* on the defensive, with your opponent running *you* from side to side and up and back, that's *war,* so stay down. The more aggressive the game is, the lower your profile has got to be, for extra stability and power.

Most of the time you're either going to be on the baseline or up at the net, except for approach shots and half-volleys. Obviously, the closer you come to the net, the quicker the action is, because the ball has less time and distance to travel before it reaches you. This means you have to be in a more intense ready position as you come in. Make sure you set up before your opponent hits the ball; when you go after it, you want to feel like a leopard pouncing on a deer from up in a tree.

Being up at net is the quickest, most aggressive part of any tennis match because there's so little time between the moment the ball is hit and when it gets to you. There's no time to fool around at net. Once you're up there you have exactly *half* the time to prepare that you do on the baseline, so you have to be on your toes and twice as ready, whether you're playing singles or doubles; the net is where it *is* in doubles. You must be in position to respond with catlike quickness and no hesitation whatsoever. The ball will be coming in hard and fast, so your timing, coordination, and alertness must be as perfect as you can make them. Your reactions have to be reflexive: the instant you see the ball hit, you respond. It comes in much harder at net than at the baseline, since it loses a lot of its pace after it bounces, so you have to be very stable. If you're really getting blasted, lower your center of gravity and widen your base—never getting too wide to move, though. Staying low at net will also help you to "sight" the ball better— will give you a better perspective on it—and keep you alert for net cords and dink shots. People often get in such high gear up at net that they flub the soft stuff.

A lot of professional players move back and forth, doing a bouncing little dance, when they're at net. That's nerves—getting ready to unleash, spring, and react one way or the other. You never see good players guessing wrong when it comes to this constant motion at net, because there's never any commission of balance; they always maintain their equal profiles. It's not to get a head start on the ball, or to try to guess where it's going, but

merely to keep their feet vibrant and alive, ready to go, then—
Boom!—they're on their way. The alternative is standing pat, dead
in the ground, just there, theoretically in great position but not
really ready for the shot—aware of the ball and the racket but not
of the feet.

When you're at net, remember to maintain your ready position
until the point is over. In other words, if you have to hit a low
volley, maintain your aggressive profile by bending mainly at the
knees—don't just drop your head or the head of your racket—and
come back up afterward. If you have to raise up to hit a high
volley, remember to recover low and forward again.

EIGHT-SECOND DRILL

Now that you have a good ready/recovery/return-of-serve position—weight low and in front—I want you to get in position
and to move your feet in place as quickly as you can for eight
seconds. Running in place is usually done with high knees, but
in this quick-step drill only lift your feet four or five inches off
the ground—just pick each one up and put it down as quickly
as possible. Keep your arms tucked into your body and land on
the balls of your feet. Keep count by tens because (I hope) you'll
be going too fast to count each step. When twenty or thirty
people are doing this drill all at once in my clinic, it sounds
something like an office full of typists. You should be doing about
forty-five per eight seconds at first; try to work up to seventy to
a hundred eventually.

Now get down even lower and try the drill again. You should
be even quicker this time. Notice the position your body is in
in order for your feet to move quickly. You'll never have to run
this way when you play; I mean, nobody takes four-inch strides
on the tennis court. I just want you to realize exactly how quickly
your feet can move when they put their minds to it. A lot of
people who have trouble covering the court when they play think
it's because they have slow, heavy, leaden feet. Actually, the
human body is designed better for *speed* then it is for strength.
The reason most "slow" people clunk around on the court is that
they are totally untrained in the techniques of efficient motion.

If you try this experiment, I'll show you what I mean. Do the same Eight-Second Drill again, only this time stand up tall and let your *heels* hit the ground first as you run in place. You'll probably notice that your feet move much more slowly this way —a basic positional change and your score most likely decreases by something like a full quarter. Yet this is the way so many people play tennis—up tall and on their heels.

Lots of people run heel-toe, heel-toe, just like they walk. This is absolutely wrong; you simply cannot run quickly on your heels, as you just saw. You want to lead with your toes, which means you have to run with *forward lean.* Try running on your toes with your weight behind you; you'll have a tough time. And vice versa: if your weight is in front of you, you can't run on your heels; your toes will lead automatically. If you're hitting on your heels when you run, either your weight is too far back, or you're taking too long a stride. But you're in good company: I used to catch Ashe landing on his heels all the time, and Tanner used to run on his whole foot, as though his feet were made of lead.

Actually, when you run, you should land on the balls of your feet—on the front third. What happens is that after you land, you roll back onto your whole foot, and then you roll forward again onto the front of your foot, to push off. This all happens too quickly for you to be aware of it when you're running, but if you try it in slow motion you'll see what I mean.

When I show this drill to people who have been running a certain way all their lives, sometimes someone complains, "How can you expect me to relearn to run at this stage of the game?" Let me explain that I'm not trying to redesign your entire running style, just to polish it up. You should definitely work with what you've got. Just as everyone walks differently because of different builds, weight distributions, leg lengths, and so on, everyone runs differently, too. Only make the changes that are necessary in your running style, because running is a natural activity. You don't want to interfere with your own rhythm and coordination and end up with paralysis by analysis.

The next time you're playing tennis and having trouble getting to your opponent's shots, take a look at how you're running; you're probably up tall—what Tanner calls "spectating"—and landing on your heels. Get some *forward lean* and a *toe lead*, and see how many more of those balls you'll reach. You'll turn some of your opponent's good shots into *your* great gets.

4 ⊙ Stride Pattern

The Eight-Second Drill shows you just how quickly you can move your feet, but running in place won't get you very far on the tennis court. The foundation of efficient running is a good *stride pattern,* the maximum-length stride you can take on a court, whatever surface it may be, and still maintain a toe lead. If your strides are too short, you'll take choppy little steps that won't get you anywhere. A stride that's too long will land you on your heels with every step, which, as you just learned, is a very slow way to move on the court. A too-long stride also causes another common error, which is to shorten up to a mincing little dance as you get close to the ball.

The fifteen-year-old girl who plays number one on her school tennis team has asthma and used to get winded quickly when she played tennis. Learning to run with a stride that's neither too long nor too short has made her more efficient; she can accomplish more with less effort and no longer gets all tired out when she plays. Another woman who took my clinic, who used to run flat-footed, had a weak left ankle that doesn't give her trouble anymore. She believes learning to run properly has helped strengthen it. But you don't have to have medical problems to benefit from a good stride pattern.

It's not just amateurs who run incorrectly. Charles Pasarell used to start off with one great huge step until we worked on his stride pattern. He and some of the other guys have discovered that shortening their strides helps them get a quicker start, be better balanced when they make contact with the ball, and recover more quickly. Learning a good stride pattern can do as much for your tennis game as learning to volley effectively.

Different court surfaces require different stride patterns. Clay, for example, which is soft and doesn't offer very good footing, takes a slightly shorter stride than a hard, fast surface like asphalt or cement. More on that later. Right now we'll assume you're playing on some type of hard, fast court. To figure out your stride pattern, you'll need a tennis court, five markers (tennis balls will do but adhesive tape would be better), a tape measure, and a friend.

1. Walk off eight normal steps from the baseline toward the net and mark the spot with a ball or a piece of tape. Walk it again— eight normal steps as though you were walking down the street. If the distance changes, adjust the marker. Walk it three times before making your final mark. Then, to add an extra nine or ten inches, place your racket head directly in front of your mark, parallel to the net, and mark the spot. Clear away the other marks.

2. Starting with your toes exactly on the baseline, run from the baseline to your mark, trying to take the distance in exactly five strides. But don't take two long and then three short steps just to hit the mark. You're trying to measure your stride pattern, and if you're overshooting the mark, your strides are too long, so shorten them up stride by stride. Your five strides shouldn't be equal in length, though, because your strides lengthen as you pick up speed. For this reason, run from the baseline to the mark, then walk back to the baseline and try again, instead of trying to work from both ends.

It may take you as many as ten run-throughs to get it perfect: five natural, smooth, toe-leading strides, landing right on the

(*Above*) Have your friend mark off each stride at the point where your toe hits the ground. (*Below*) Run through your stride pattern as many times as you need to get it perfect.

money without having to adjust one way or the other. Practice it until you can hit the mark every time. Run through it slowly, just as you hit your strokes slowly when you were learning to groove them. Don't point your toes out when you run, making chicken tracks, and don't run pigeon-toed, pointing them in. You should run like an Indian walks, toes pointed straight ahead.

3. When you can hit the spot every time, have your friend mark off each of your strides at the point where your toe hits the ground. It will probably take one complete run-through to mark off each stride. Don't just run two steps, now, and cut off, because people have a tendency to take really short strides when they do that. Run the whole five steps each time and have your friend mark only one at a time.

That's your stride pattern. Between the first two strides, the increase might be as much as a foot; between the other three, a few inches each. Measure the first two strides with the tape measure because they're the most important; it's essential that your stride pattern be perfect when you're getting your body in motion. Run through your whole stride pattern fifteen, twenty, even thirty times, until you get the first two steps exactly right every single time, so you know precisely how far your feet have to move from the first step to the second step.

Just as you groove your strokes before you play a match, take a minute or two to groove your stride pattern on the court, particularly when you're in a tournament or any other situation when you want to play your best. Write the measurements of the first two steps on your racket cover—*39 44;* or *48 56*—whatever it happens to be. Then, before an important match, mark off your first two strides with a tape measure and run through them several times, so that everything will be grooved in—your feet, your strokes, and, I hope, your head.

5 ⓪ Court Surfaces

A lot of players lose matches by playing all surfaces the same way. If you're used to playing on a fast court like asphalt or grass, you've probably developed a serve-and-volley game. If you play on a slow court like clay or Har-tru, you probably play a baseline game. Even most pros have a favorite surface, generally the one they grew up on. There are pros who usually go far in tournaments they play on fast courts and consistently get put out in the first or second round on clay.

The speed of a court refers to how the ball reacts when it comes off the surface. On clay, where the ball takes a high, slow, uniform bounce, you have almost a whole extra second to get to it than you do on grass, which means that on clay it's possible to run down practically everything, even shots that would be outright winners on grass. Court surfaces also vary in how much traction they give you, how slippery they are, and whether they "give" under your feet. You can't move exactly the same way on different surfaces. Making some adjustments in your stride pattern and your court posture will help you stay balanced and steady on whatever surface you're playing, so the court doesn't become your opponent and you get to your shots in time and under control.

39

Grass is one of the fastest surfaces. The ball takes a low bounce on grass—and if the grass isn't in top shape, it frequently takes a bad bounce—and then it just dies. If it's hit hard, the ball skids. Grass is the hardest surface for someone with a slow-court game to move on effectively. What would be an easy baseline rally on clay is a much faster, harder situation on grass, partly because players tend to hit bigger on fast courts. Because grass is soft and gives, it's easy on your legs. But it's also slippery, and even more so after rain or watering. Once you get committed one way or the other, it's extremely hard to change direction—you're moving aggressively and there's very little friction to help you stop, so you have to be especially conscious of stopping and setting up early. You'll have a lot of problems on grass if you're not in perfect balance and if your stride pattern isn't right on the money.

All this means that grass, like any fast surface, requires an active participation between you and your profile. You should stay lower than usual and shorten your stride pattern slightly. The formula for a hard court—eight walking steps plus one racket head divided by five running steps—should be modified to eight walking steps even divided by five running steps.

Cement and asphalt are also usually very fast courts with no give whatsoever, which makes them easy surfaces to run on: you can really take off. People who have good net games usually love to play on hard courts because they can come right in and nail you. You need a fast-game profile for a hard court: keep low and as you come up to net, be ready to be ready. The stride pattern for cement and asphalt is the one you learned on page 36—eight plus one divided by five.

There are so many different synthetic surfaces now that it's impossible to generalize much about them, but as a rule, they are slower than grass and faster than clay, and usually fast enough to favor the attacker. Most of these courts give you good traction and firm footing, so stopping and changing direction quickly are no problem if you keep your balance. Your stride pattern should be eight plus one divided by five, just as on asphalt and cement.

On clay, you don't want as aggressive a profile or as long a stride as on the other surfaces. You should play a hair taller on clay, because if you're too low and too far forward, your feet will just spin right out, like tires with bald treads. The stride-pattern formula for clay is eight walking steps *minus* one racket head divided by five running steps. The few-inches-per-stride difference will enable you to keep your footing and to cut down on excess sliding.

Ashe says that playing on clay feels like playing on roller skates, but to move well on clay, you have to slide. Sliding into the ball will keep you from overrunning it, will get you to the ball on the correct foot, and will help you recover and change direction more quickly for the next ball. If you run hard, you'll slide naturally. Most clay-court players slide two or three feet into their shots, some pros as much as six feet. To slide on long, hard runs, keep your back foot steady when you're coming into the ball and slide your front foot into position. Remember to stay squared away for good balance.

Har-tru, which is a crushed-rock surface, plays a lot like clay but a bit faster, and requires the same profile and stride pattern. You'll slide on Har-tru just like on clay. When either clay or Har-tru has just been watered or rained on, it will play slower and softer than when it's dry.

6 ⚾ Footwork into the Inner and Outer Ball

First let's distinguish between two positions of the ball: the inner ball, which is one that you can reach comfortably without trying too hard, and the outer ball, which is one you really have to run for. There are also all those balls that land somewhere in between these two extremes; in fact, these are probably the majority of balls you'll come up against in a match.

The easiest ball to hit is the one that comes right to you. This doesn't happen very many times in a match, and when it does, probably you can almost always hit a great shot back. Any ball that you can get to and set up for early enough to hit *as if* it had come right to you, giving you the opportunity to make a controlled, offensive shot, is an inner ball. It's no set distance away; everybody has a particular range in which he's comfortable and can move well. Whether a ball is within your range also depends on its speed, its spin, and the type of court surface you're playing on.

Inner balls are the ones you can't afford to louse up. There is never any excuse for hitting an inner ball on the run. It's your bread-and-butter shot because it gives you your best opportunity to hit the best shot you know how to make. But a lot of players get lazy on inner balls, saying to themselves, "Well, it's a close ball, easy to reach, so I'll just lope over there and hit it," instead of getting there, setting up as early as possible, and going for a big shot. Also, they'll often play inner balls too close to their bodies instead of moving a racket-length away. It's when the ball lands within your range that you're most likely to play a lazy shot.

The critical phase of the footwork into the inner ball is the final adjustments you make to set yourself up perfectly for your shot. Get quickly to the approximately correct position, moving according to the flight of the ball, using a burst of speed if necessary. Get side-on to the net, and as the ball bounces, make the final adjustments that will allow you to control your shot completely—whatever weight shifts you need, or little steps back or in, up or down necessary to hit the ball at your most comfortable level, probably waist-high. The most important thing is to end up with your back foot, the one nearest the fence, planted,

Footwork, forehand inner ball: back foot planted . . . uncoil and shift your weight forward as you attack the ball in front of you.

Footwork, backhand inner ball: back foot planted . . . uncoil and shift forward as you attack the ball in front of you.

because it's transferring your weight from your back foot to your front foot, the one nearest the net, that provides the power source for your stroke. As you hit, you uncoil and shift your weight forward onto your front foot, and attack the ball in front of you.

The farther away the ball is, the less time you're going to have to set up perfectly for it. For balls that land in a category somewhere between inner balls and outer balls, you probably won't have time to make those final adjustments, but if you hustle, you usually will have time to stop, plant your back foot, and step into the ball.

The Outer Ball: Getting a Quick Start

You're standing in ready position at the center of the baseline. Your opponent hits the ball wide to your forehand. You've got a

lot of ground to cover. You get your racket back and start running, right? Wrong.

When there are five, six, seven, or even more running steps
between you and the ball, there's absolutely no reason in the
world to get your racket back on the first step. Not only is it
unnecessary, it's a hindrance. A racket extended behind you when
you're trying to get started to run down a long ball is like trying
to beat out a bunt with the bat in your hand. The two activities
—getting to the ball and hitting it—have to be separated. Remember that this applies only to the outside ball, the one that
requires a lot of running. The first thing you've got to do is to
overcome the inertia of being stationary and get your body in
motion. After the first two steps, when you've established your
momentum, *then* you're ready to start thinking about hitting the
ball.

The key to reaching that wide forehand on time is pushing off
—getting a quick start. Whereas the critical part of inner-ball
footwork is at the end, the critical part of outer-ball footwork is
at the beginning. As Tom Gorman notes, saving half or even just
a tenth of a second here can often mean the difference between a
defensive and an offensive shot.

The reason you want your weight forward when you're in
ready position is that the closer your center of gravity is to the
front edge of your base of support, the more quickly you can get
started. What actually happens when you run is that first your
body moves out in front of your feet, which puts you off-balance.
Then you bring your foot forward to regain your balance, then
you move forward out in front of your feet again, and so on.
Running is moving forward by continually losing and recovering
your balance.

Let's get back to that wide forehand. You're in good ready
position on the baseline—low, forward, and on your toes. As
soon as you see that your opponent has hit to your forehand, the
first thing you have to do is pivot by turning your whole body
in the direction in which you're going, dropping your weight
lower and farther forward, and *as you're turning,* push off. The

Pivot: as you're turning, push off.

pivot and push-off have to be simultaneous, not sequential.

For these first two momentum-establishing steps, your legs have to feel like springs, with only your toes hitting the ground. The rhythm of these first two steps is very quick: ONE-TWO!—as fast as you can say it; not one, two. It's TOE-TOE!—an explosive motion, because the faster you can get started, the faster you'll go.

Your weight should be way out in front of yourself, and very low—low enough to get under a racket held at waist-height. This low start will get you off the mark a lot more quickly. That's why sprinters start from a crouch.

Try this with a friend: have him hold a racket level with your waist, and you take off under it—ONE-TWO! You've got to get under the racket, not by stooping but by getting your weight way out in front of your lead knee. You may think this position is *too* low and *too* far forward, but it's not. It's by far the most efficient way to get your weight working for you instead of against you, allowing it to pull you forward rather than having to muscle it through.

Using Your Arms

To get your body in the right motion to chase down a ball, you have to realize that when your feet take a step, your arms should move in conjunction with them. Since they are attached to your body, you might as well let them help you get going.

Most people don't use their arms at all when they run on the tennis court, and many players who use them do so incorrectly, muscling them or sticking their elbows out as though they're beating a drum. The following method for learning the correct arm action will let you maintain your particular natural motion.

Start by standing up straight, with your arms at your sides. Let them swing back and forth, approximately up to shoulder height. When one arm is at the top of its upswing, hold it up there and let the other one keep swinging a few more times. Now bend your swinging arm at the elbow, not locking it but keeping it firm

Friend holds a racket level with your waist . . . and you take off under it, getting your weight way out in front of your lead knee.

(*Left*) Hold one arm at the top of the upswing, keep swinging the other one. (*Center*) Bend your swinging arm at the elbow, firm but not locked. (*Right*) Let your arms swing together.

enough so that it's not floppy. Keep it swinging. Now bend the one hanging up in the air, and let your arms swing together. Now make it quicker: pump them ONE-TWO, ONE-TWO, as fast as you can say it and as fast as you can do it—just like the first two steps. You'll notice that your elbows are not sticking out, nor are they tucked in too tight. They're pumping right alongside your body. Notice also that your hands are going only as high as your chin in front of you and back only as far as your hips; no more, no less. The reason we have such an abbreviated arm swing is that you'll be taking relatively short, quick steps. If you were going to take a long stride, you would need a long arm swing. But that's track, not tennis. Tennis requires a somewhat shorter motion in your arms as well as in your feet.

You'll have one hand free when you're pumping on these first two steps. You don't want it either clenched tight or floppy and loose. If you close it around three fingers of the other hand, and then take the fingers out, that's a good position: relaxed and comfortable and firm.

Let your racket become an extension of your arm for these first two steps. Hold it firmly and pump your arm naturally as if the racket were not in your hand. Don't move it around excessively because any resistance will affect your momentum a great deal.

Your arm action should balance your legs. Since every action has an equal and opposite reaction, when your arm goes back, your body goes forward. When you run, start pumping with the arm opposite the lead leg. In other words, when the left leg leads, the right arm leads. I'll get into exactly which leg leads when in a moment.

QUICK-START HARNESS DRILL

This drill will help you develop the power and control you need to generate speed for the first two steps of a long run.

Hold onto your racket. Put a towel around your waist and have a friend stand behind you holding the ends. As you pull forward— staying low, on your toes, and driving with your arms—have him pull back on you hard enough so that you can pull him into a walk, but not a run. Take short, quick, aggressive steps—it should take you about fifteen steps to get from the baseline to the service line —a distance of eighteen feet, if you're doing this off the court.

If your body is too high, you'll just dance off your feet and get what I call the rainbow effect, a high arc that dissipates all your power. Drive your feet across with a forward, pushing action with each step, which will help you keep your weight down and in front. Try to maintain the ONE-TWO rhythm, keeping it smooth, solid, and aggressive.

If you're running hard but not moving forward, your partner is pulling back too hard and should ease up a bit. If you can pull him into a run, he's not pulling back hard enough. He has to stay low, too, keeping a wide base, bending at the knees, and sitting back in his seat so he can provide enough resistance. You stay low and forward, he stays low and back. You're both doing it

Quick-Start Harness Drill: Stay low, on your toes, and pump with your arms.

correctly if he's pulling back hard, you're running full-strength, and he's only walking.

After you've got it right, try it without the towel. Keep your ONE-TWO rhythm, but now try to maintain your stride pattern, too. You should shoot right out of there. Sometimes in my clinics I'll whisper, "Let it go," to the person holding the towel. The runner takes off like a shot. He also finds out very quickly that he'd fall flat on his face if he didn't pump with his arms, which pull him right out of trouble. Remember that you drive with the arm opposite the driving leg.

Work on getting better at it, stronger and looser. You'll find that this drill will help you get started a lot more quickly if you do it correctly and practice it. It's really just a matter of bringing out what you already have. Most players' brains usually work faster than their feet, and the Harness Drill can improve the communication between them.

After the first two explosive steps, you're on your way. Once you've established your momentum, it will take care of itself if you maintain your toe lead, your forward lean, and your stride pattern. Now you can concentrate completely on preparing to hit the ball.

On the third step, begin to rise up into your basic hitting position, and begin to get your racket back. You're down really low for the first two steps; don't pop up suddenly, or pull your racket back all at once, because that would throw your weight back and you'd be running on your heels. Rise up gradually, reacting to the level of the ball. Your racket should be all the way back one step before your last running step so you'll have as much time as possible to plant your feet, set up, and make a great get. If you end up having to hit the ball on the run despite having gotten a quick start and maintaining your stride pattern, well, you probably wouldn't have reached it at all any other way.

PIVOTING: RUNNING CROSS-COURT—LEG LEADS

Let's get back to the question of which foot to lead with when you're going after an outer ball. To change direction on the tennis court, you have to pivot, which simply means turn, and simultaneously take your first step. It's very important to take that first step with the correct foot, so that you can transfer your weight forward, keep a toe lead, and end up hitting off the correct foot. Leading with the wrong foot would prevent you from doing anything worthwhile with your weight, you'd get a slow start, and you'd most likely get to the ball on the wrong foot.

When you're running to the right, whether you're right-handed or left-handed, your first step should be with your left foot. This is a *left-leg lead*. When you're running to the left, your right leg leads. In other words, the leg closest to the net as you pivot is always the leg that leads in running down a long ball. And you start pumping with the opposite arm.

When I teach the pivots in my clinics, it usually takes a while before everyone gets them right. Even though it's just like walking —left arm, right leg, and vice versa—a lot of people have trouble

(*Above*) Pivoting: left leg, right arm lead. (*Below*) Pivoting: right leg, left arm lead.

with it at first, leading with the wrong arm, or the wrong leg, or both. So we walk through each pivot a few times first to get the feel and the correct arm-and-leg coordination. Then we do them over and over, from sideline to sideline, to simulate cross-court shots. By the time the people leave the clinic, everyone knows how to pivot, and no one has to waste any more time starting on the wrong foot.

Stand in ready position on the deuce court sideline. Pretend you've just been drawn wide. You can expect the next shot to go cross-court. Pivot, drop, push off, and run cross-court to the ad court sideline, remembering your stride pattern, keeping your weight in front, and keeping a toe lead. From the deuce court sideline, it's right leg, left arm; from the ad court sideline, left leg, right arm.

Take the time to learn the pivots properly and practice them until they're habitual, because when you're playing in a match you're concentrating on outsmarting your opponent and winning points; there's no time to think about technique, either for strokes or footwork. I know one woman who practiced those leg leads until she could almost do them in her sleep. Then when she took a Latin dance class and the rest of the class had a lot of trouble with the steps that required similar footwork, for her it had become second nature. I also know a guy who, instead of jogging, runs through the pivots in the park before he plays, so he gets in some footwork practice as he's warming up.

GETTING DROP SHOTS

The secret to not getting drop-shotted is going after the ball with no hesitation whatsoever. In that split second when you're deciding *Can I make it or can't I?*—you've probably already blown it. Faith in your own quickness and getting into the habit of reacting immediately to every ball will get you to shots you never thought you could reach.

Several years ago, when I was working out with a group of tennis professionals in Puerto Rico, we clocked drop shots to see how long they took to go over the net, bounce, and go out of play. The average drop shot took 1.8 seconds on clay. It should take you between 1 and 1.5 seconds to run from the baseline to the net if you can get off the mark quickly and run half-way decently—which gives you time to spare. For the pros, this was a real revelation; I convinced them that there was no drop shot they should miss. South African player Ray Moore told me, "Now every time a guy drop-shots me, I always go flat out for it. I wouldn't say that I haven't missed one since then, but at least I have the confidence to try for it." The woman who prac-ticed her pivots so diligently told me that her tennis friends used to say, "All we have to do to win the point is drop-shot her." Though she had the strokes, she couldn't get to the ball; she would just say "Good shot" from the baseline instead of running it down. Once she had learned how to react automatically and get off on the right foot, she wasn't a victim anymore. She just hadn't realized before that she could move so quickly. I've no-ticed that, in general, women find moving forward more difficult than moving to the sides, so this is something they particularly should work on.

To move cross-court, you have to change direction by pivot-ing. But to get to a drop shot from the baseline, there's no need to pivot, since you're already facing the direction in which you have to go—forward. However, the leg leads for running down drop shots are identical to the leg leads for cross-court shots: your right leg leads going toward the ad court, your left leg leads going toward the deuce court, so that your weight is working for you by pulling your body forward. The arm work is also the same. And just as when you're running cross-court, you really have to dig out after that drop shot by dropping your weight way down and in front of your lead knee, like in the Harness Drill.

I've noticed that in starting to move forward, many players have a natural tendency to *double step:* in an attempt to push off they will take a tiny, three-inch step backward before going forward. What happens is that they straighten up first when they see that the ball has been hit, they get caught off-balance, and then they take that little step back to regain their balance. This brings their weight too far back to allow them to get down and forward quickly, and so they get to the ball late. Being in good ready position to begin with, with your weight forward enough, will prevent you from taking that unnecessary little step backward. You'll get a quicker start, and you'll make it to that drop shot in good time.

Another problem a lot of players have in running down drop shots is running through their shots, because they're moving so aggressively that they're not able to stop once they get there. This is also usually the result of starting off tall and late, and then having to generate speed throughout the fifth, sixth, and seventh steps in order to get to the ball, which means you're still accelerating while you're hitting, making it impossible to cut off quickly. The only way to avoid running through your shot is to get started quickly, and to get there early enough to stop and set up. Now, I know this isn't always possible; sometimes you're going to race in for a too-good drop shot and run into the net and lose the point. But most of the time you can get there early enough if you don't hesitate, if you stay low and if you maintain your stride pattern. Remember to slide into drop shots on clay, which will save you crucial time.

FOOTWORK AT NET

When you're up at the net, the action is often so fast that you don't have time to think about correct footwork. You're trying to volley the ball aggressively out in front of you, and frequently agility and sharp reactions are going to be your main assets.

A lot of the problems players have at net result simply from being too close to it, not allowing themselves enough time to react to the ball. This probably comes from emulating the pros, who can camp right on top of the net because they're able to handle the speed of play up there. Try to make a realistic assessment of how good a volleyer you are, and stay back far enough to give yourself a chance to do some harm. Most average players are probably best off standing midway between the service line and the net. That's far enough back so you have time to react to the ball, and close enough to hit a good, deep volley.

What's essential to effective volleying is maintaining your good ready position between each shot. Physically it's the same ready position as on the baseline, but mentally you have to be much more alert and aggressive. Keeping your toes bouncing or skipping a bit may help keep you ultravigilant and ready to pounce at net, but unless you're psychic, keep an equal profile and don't commit your weight before your opponent hits his shot. Usually having to take one huge, lunging step for an inner ball up at net is the result of being committed the wrong way: you think the ball is going to the right, it goes to the left, and you just do whatever you can to get across there. Since your balance is going one way and the ball is going the other way, you have to throw everything to the other side. Your opponent loves to see you lunging like that at net because you're telling him that you have absolutely no control whatsoever over what he's doing to you up there. Recovering immediately, staying on your toes, and maintaining an equal profile will cut down substantially on those situations and you won't get passed so easily anymore.

An inner ball at net is often an opportunity to volley the ball away, and the correct footwork can help insure it. It's standard cross-over footwork: if the ball is to your left, step forward and across with your right foot as you volley: ONE!—quick and crisp. If it's to your right, step into it with your left and BOOM!

Often you have time for good footwork even on an outer ball if the ball hasn't been hit too hard. Use the same pivots you'd use anywhere else on the court, bringing your outside leg across first. The main difference is that at net you don't want to drop down as low or to have as extreme a weight transfer as for a drop shot or a cross-court shot, because you've got to stay up to hit the ball. Elsewhere on the court, you're only concerned with getting in motion when you pivot.

More than anything else, your previous shot is going to determine what your opponent will hit back at, to, past, or over you. If you make a really good volley, you don't have to worry; with a reasonably good shot, you'll most likely get a reasonably good shot back, one that you can probably handle if you maintain your balance and react quickly enough. If you hit a weak shot, you're a sitting duck; be ready for the ball to go down the line or across the court. Take your pick. You'll be lucky just to get your racket on it by taking a flying leap and throwing yourself at the ball. The more agile you are, the more likely you are to get away with it.

OVER YOUR HEAD—GETTING LOBS

Although the overhead stroke itself is similar to the serve, the rules for getting to the ball when it sails over your head are the same as for any other shot, only more so, because the overhead is a power shot and you need every ounce of leverage you can get: a defensively hit overhead usually means disaster for you. Most missed and weak overheads are caused by not getting ready properly. If you're running forward when your opponent throws up a lob, you're stuck; you have to slam down on your heels to stop and it's virtually impossible for you to get back there in time. You should be on your toes and stationary while your opponent is hitting, so that when you see the ball lofting you can start to move back instantly. If the lob isn't very deep, the best way to retreat is by turning your body sideways to the net and backpedaling. Stay sideways until after you've made the shot. Cock your racket behind you as you begin to backpedal, because cocking it at the last second completely fouls up most people's timing. Keep your eye on the ball at all times and sight it—line it up—with your free hand.

If the lob is deep—more than six or seven steps—backpedaling would be too slow. You've got to pivot 180 degrees—turning your back to the net—drop, and run. If you have any doubts about your ability to back up for the lob, even if it's shallow, don't waste any time thinking about it—just turn around and go. Always turn in the direction in which the ball is going: if it's hit over your left shoulder, for example, pivot and follow it to the left, keeping your eye on it as best you can over your shoulder. You've really got to race it back, beating it to the spot. Get there before it bounces, going back farther than necessary so that you can set up with the ball in front of you for more leverage and better control. It's also much easier to adjust forward than to go farther back at the last moment. Overheads are always taken as forehands if it's possible, because very few people can hit backhand overheads with any power; so get set with the ball to your forehand side even if it's hit to your backhand.

If you watch tennis tournaments, you've probably seen some of the pros backpedal straight back, then jump up as they hit their overheads. This shot looks spectacular, but it takes perfect timing, and the additional leverage you'd get from hitting this way just isn't worth giving up a safer shot for. You should try to keep at least one foot on the ground when you hit an overhead, getting your leverage from being sideways to the net. The only time to jump up off the ground for an overhead is when you're at net and can only reach it by leaping up for it, or if you've mistimed the ball and have no other choice.

RETURN OF SERVE

So many people wait for that serve as though their lives were on trial. They mess up their returns because they're intimidated, and because they don't know what to do with their feet and bodies when they see the ball coming at them.

When you're receiving serve, you have certain advantages; capitalize on them. You have plenty of time to get ready before your opponent is allowed to serve; you're stationary, which makes timing the ball simpler; and you know that the ball can only land within a certain clearly defined area, the service box.

On the other hand, the serve (together with the overhead) is the fastest, hardest-hit shot in tennis—ninety to ninety-five miles an hour is not uncommon for a good male club player—and it can come in spinning, sliced, or flat. This requires the ultimate ready position: a solid base; a low, forward profile; and your weight in front on the balls of your feet for maximum control, balance, and quickness.

If you were to receive serve with your feet together, your knees stiff, your weight back, and flatfooted (which is how an awful lot of people wait for serves), you'd get blown away by a hard serve. As much as possible, you want to be like a wall when that ball comes barreling in. The harder your opponent's serve, the lower you have to be, because a hard-hit ball is generally a low one. It's also a lot easier to come up if necessary than to drop down when time is very short.

Most of the problems people have returning serve are the result of reacting too slowly. Especially on the backhand, many players wait for the ball to come to them before they get completely set up, and then suddenly it's right on top of them and they have to cramp their shots. To be in a position to react quickly, you should be waiting at the cutoff point, midway between the possible extreme lines of flight of the ball. If the server is right-handed, his serve is going to curve out in the deuce court, and toward the center in the ad court. Therefore, to receive his serve in the deuce court, you should stand approximately two feet to the left of the intersection of the singles line and the baseline, and in the ad court, midway between the center line and the singles line/baseline intersection. To receive a lefty's serve, it's just the opposite: stand approximately in the middle when he's serving into the deuce court, and approximately two feet to the right of the singles line in the ad court.* You should be as close in an possible (sometimes four feet behind the baseline is as close as possible), for several reasons: (a) If you can get the ball on the rise, it won't have developed all its spin yet. (b) You'll also be putting pressure on the server, giving him less time to prepare for his next shot, or to get to the net, which gives you a chance to hit a better-than-adequate return. (c) Also, the closer you are to the net for your return, the better angle you can get

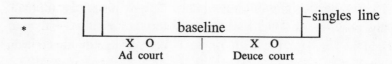

Key
O: receiving a right-handed person's serve
X: receiving a left-handed person's serve

on your shot, and the faster you can get in to net. This goes for both your opponent's first and second serves; obviously it's easier to accomplish on his second, which will have less pace and often less depth.

The *instant* you see to which side the ball is coming, shift your weight to that side and get your racket back. The footwork for return of serve is exactly the same as for any other shot. If it's an inner ball, coming in to your right side (whether it's a backhand or a forehand will depend on whether you're right- or left-handed), it's a right-leg plant and then step forward into the ball with your left. If it's outside your range to the right, then it's a left-leg lead, so that, again, you wind up planting your right foot and stepping into the ball with your left. If you're going to be hitting off your left side, left-leg plant for an inner ball, right-leg lead for an outer ball.

When I teach this return-of-serve footwork, sometimes I get a lot of backtalk at first: "Who's got time to think about all this footwork, Hines, when the ball's coming at me a million miles an hour?" Well, all I can say is, you've got to do *something* with your feet, so you might as well do something *right* with them. People usually come around to my way of thinking after a while, when they see that it works.

What should you be doing while your opponent is winding up to serve? While you're waiting for that serve, you don't necessarily have to be still. You can do whatever feels comfortable and keeps you relaxed, as long as you don't give anything up. An easy sway back and forth might ease the tension for you and help you concentrate, the way a cobra sways its head before it gets ready to strike. Some people, especially beginners, move excessively, just imitating what they see more experienced players doing without really getting any benefit from it themselves. Don't bounce or sway so much that you risk getting caught off-balance. How much is too much? If you're bouncing up and down and are in the air when the server hits the ball, that's too much.

Remember always to recover after you return serve. I often see players hit a good return and then just stand there admiring their own shot, sure that it's a winner. Then while they're standing there straight up and flat-footed, the ball comes whizzing back and they're not ready for it. Always assume the ball is coming back and going in until the point is over.

7 ⊕ Putting It All Together

The major goal of this book is to help you improve your court mobility so that you can reach practically any ball that comes over the net with the control and balance necessary to making the best shot you're capable of hitting, rather than either missing it altogether or having to struggle, hit from a bad position, and just hope the ball goes over and in because you lost so much time getting to it. The techniques and drills in this book are designed to help you expand your *comfort range,* the area in which you can move easily and hit solid, offensive shots.

When the ball is within your comfort range (what I've been calling the inner ball), whether it's in front of you, behind you, or to either side, you can get there in plenty of time to set up, plant your feet before you swing, and attack it in front of you, getting your weight into your shot. The limits of your comfort range are defined by where you have to start struggling to get to the ball and are forced to hit it defensively. You probably find that your range varies from day to day. Some days your timing is off, you're a little sluggish, your feet just won't move, or whatever; range depends not only on your *ability* to move but also on your *confidence* and *motivation* to go after a particular ball: the more you go for, the more you get.

Most average players have a range of about eight feet to either side and behind them, and twelve to fifteen feet in front of them. Obviously, advanced players have a greater range, a greater ability to cover the court, than beginners. But practically all tennis players are better at stroking the ball than at moving for it, because if you have to move at the same time the ball is moving, the timing is much more complicated than if you're stationary. No matter how good your strokes are, you're always going to be in trouble on the court unless motion is working for you. Motion and footwork problems, more than anything else, are what make second-rate players second-rate.

No one's range covers every extremity of the court. Even Jimmy Connors gets drawn off the court once in a while and can't get back in time for a shot hit to the other side. But nothing will shake your opponent's confidence more than watching you race over and attack his "winner." He'll think there's *nothing* you can't get to, and he'll start wondering what he has to do to the damn ball to get one past you—and then watch him start making errors trying.

If you want to increase your comfort range, you should follow the five steps below for every shot. I'll deal with each one in turn.

1. Be stationary, in good ready position, at the spot on the court that will allow you the best opportunity to go after whatever your opponent can possibly hit to you, *before* your opponent hits the ball.

2. React instantly when he does hit it.

3. Move quickly according to the flight of the ball, pivoting and using your stride pattern to get to a long ball.

4. Establish your hitting position (outside leg planted, ready to come into the ball) as early as possible before you hit, making whatever final adjustments necessary to control the inner ball and hit it at your most comfortable level, probably waist-height.

5. After you make your shot, immediately recover and return to that part of the court that seems to give you an equal chance to react to and control your opponent's next shot, again remaining in your aggressive profile.

1. *Coming to a stop before your opponent hits the ball* is one of the main keys to covering the court. You may *think* you're always making progress while you're running, but it's just not true. You have your entire comfort range when you're stationary. It's practically nil while you're in motion, because your momentum is carrying you forward, making it impossible for you to stop or to change direction quickly. For example, if you're moving forward as your opponent hits the ball down the line, you'll have to career over to it—and you'll get there late and off-balance. If, instead, you are stationary and in ready position while he's hitting, you can simply pivot and run; if your balance is not committed to one side or another, you can move quickly in any direction.

Stopping and setting up before your opponent makes his shot is extremely important—whether you are receiving serve, hitting from the baseline, or volleying up at the net. One of the axioms of tennis is that after you make your shot, you've got to get back to the center of the court. I've seen players follow this rule so rigidly that they lose sight of the fact that the object of the game is to get to the *ball,* not back to the center of the court.

Let's say you've just returned a wide forehand. If you're running back to the center and your opponent drills away at the same spot again, you're obviously going to get caught going the wrong way. You're back in position but the ball is somewhere else. You get an A for theory, for being where you're "supposed" to be, but an F for losing the point—you've played the court rather than the ball. Instead, you should have made your shot, run as far back to the cutoff spot—the spot that will give you your best chance to go after your opponent's next shot, which is usually (but not always) the center of the baseline or net—as possible, and stopped and established an aggressive ready position before your opponent made his shot. Then, even if you've only gotten halfway back to the center, you're in a better position to reach a ball hit behind you, and you are also in an excellent starting position to pivot and drive out quickly if he has hit to your backhand. Your weight commitment is just as important as how far you are from the ball in determining whether or not you're going to get to it, and at no time is your weight more committed than when you're running.

It's a matter of percentages. You want to have a crack at whatever your opponent can hit to you. The moment you turn your back on a portion of the court and start running, you're giving up every step behind you. Your momentum is carrying you one way and that's the only general direction in which you're going to be effective. The greater your momentum, the more difficult it is to stop or to redirect your motion toward the ball, so even if you do have a chance to reverse your direction and get back, you're still going to have a hell of a time getting to that ball.

Sure, sometimes you have no choice. You make a weak shot, your opponent is all over it, and you just have to guess where he's likely to hit and get there, fast—it's your only chance. But most of the time you do have some degree of control over the situation, which you're just forfeiting by being on the run while your opponent is hitting the ball, hoping that his shot will go that way. Particularly if you've just made a good shot—changed the pace, gotten your opponent out of position, hit to his weakness —he's not going to be able to hit where he wants, but chances are that he *could* sneak one behind you if you gave him the opening. If you're dashing back across to the middle of the court while he's hitting the ball, you're giving up control of the point. The ball could be three feet away from you, but if you're going the wrong way, it might as well be a mile.

Certainly, if you have time, and you usually do after you hit, get back to the spot midway between the ball's possible lines of flight, the spot that allows you an equal chance of getting to whatever your opponent can hit next, whether it's a forehand, a backhand, a drop shot, or a lob, without leaving yourself an inordinate amount of territory to cover on one side and an extremely small area on another. But it's *always* preferable to give up a little territory in front of you in order to assume a solid, aggressive ready position while your opponent is hitting. Don't give up the ball for a spot on the court!

RUSHING THE NET

You're an aggressive serve-and-volleyer, or you'd like to be, and you've just hit your big, booming serve. You're flying in to the net as fast as your legs can carry you because you want to make your first volley from as close in as possible, so that you can hit the ball deep or angle it away. When your opponent hits his return you react to his shot by "splitting"—stopping your forward momentum by spreading your feet and coming down on both heels. His return is heading down the line. You lunge for it, but it's gone. Or he lobs it over your head, and you're just stuck there, screeching to a halt on your heels. Or your volley is unsteady because you are, and the ball flies out of the court.

Sound familiar? I've seen it a thousand times. "Serve and split" is probably the worst idea that ever came into tennis, because that split is always late, always in reaction to the other guy's shot. In fact, the split is nothing *but* a reaction; it's not really a position at all, and when the ball comes back you're still in that reactive stance, instead of being established and ready for the return. Here's what happens: when you're running forward, your weight is committed forward. If the ball goes a few yards to your left or right, you have to get to the side. But you can't make a sharp turn when you're moving. First you have to stop by rearing back on your heels, because to absorb your forward momentum, your center of gravity has to go back. Then you have to make a U-turn to get your weight going in the right direction, which uses up a lot of time and energy, and then more often than not you either miss the ball completely or at best hit an extremely weak shot.

Stopping in reaction to your opponent's return wastes time when time is critical. Once he hits the ball, the clock starts. A return hit fairly hard takes about half a second to go thirty feet, which isn't much time. If you're busy stopping after that return is hit, by the time you're ready to go again, a good return will be gone. If you'd stopped and set up *before* the ball was hit, be-

(*Left*) "Splitting" in reaction to opponent's return by rearing back on heels. (*Right*) Making a U-turn to get going again.

fore you had to go anywhere, all you'd have to do is start—you'd have eliminated an extra step.

Some of the pros I work with fought me like hell on this point at first, because usually they got away with flying in and splitting at the last instant. If you're a good serve-and-volleyer playing a so-so returner-of-serve, you can probably get away with it, too, because either you will force an error, or the ball will usually come within your range and you can run right through it and put it away or do something effective with it. But you've got no range whatsoever on your heels, and if you're playing against a guy who can chip those damn shots past you, or lob over your head, or hit down at your feet, then you'd better be prepared to deal with what he's dealing out to you.

If you want to use that serve-and-split effectively, you're going to have to retime it and split *before* the ball is hit, so that you can set up and be in a position to move in any direction— forward, to either side, across, or back—before your opponent makes his shot. The best way to retain the offensive on your serve is to come in aggressively until the split second before your opponent hits his return, set up, and react to the return from where

Lunging for the ball.

you are. Gain as much ground as you can; most of the time you'll be able to come in three, four, or five steps, depending on your serve—the faster your serve, the less you'll get, because you'll have less time. Someone like Tanner is lucky if he gets in three steps on grass.

When you finish your serve, you are low and forward. Follow the natural flow of your weight, letting it pull you forward. If you stay low, not straightening up after you serve, you'll be able to penetrate much farther into the court. In other words, stay down for a quick start—the same quick start as on the first two steps of a long run: ONE-TWO.

At first, you probably won't penetrate deeply enough to do much with your first volley, but even if you don't make it to the service line, learn to live with what you can get. It's preferable to give up territory for good position and stability so that you can attack the ball. In the long run, you won't be giving up any ground at all by stopping a little sooner. What will happen is that you'll be able to come in three or four steps before you have to stop and set up. While this will land you behind the service line, since your reaction to the ball will be forward, you'll end up hitting your first volley in front of the service line, just as you did when you were running through it. At the same time, you'll greatly reduce your chances of being passed or messed up by any kind of ball outside your range. As you practice it and get stronger and quicker, you'll find yourself hitting the ball with control at the same spot you were flailing to reach before.

Here's a way to break yourself of the habit of flying in to the net after you serve, running until the ball is hit, and landing on your heels with stiff knees. I've used it successfully with many pros. You'll need two friends, one to return your serve and one to watch.

First, practice serving and coming in just two steps before setting up for your friend's return, remembering to stay low after you serve to get a quick start. Running in only two steps will give you plenty of time to wait for the ball. You'll be much too far back to do anything worthwhile with it; this is just to give you the idea of setting up *before* rather than *as* the ball is hit. When you've trained yourself to stop after two steps, graduate to three. By the third or fourth step, you should be getting close to the moment the return is hit. At this point, be guided by the person watching. He should yell "Now!" as soon as he sees that the receiver is about to hit his return (to give you time to react to his voice). Stop and set up as soon as you hear the "Now!" (I've found that having a third party yell "Now" works better than having the receiver do both jobs, because it's tough to hit a good return and holler at the same time.)

Go through this exercise as many times as necessary to get the feel of it, until you can stop and set up every time before the return is hit. When you've got it right, practice it without your friend hollering "Now!" You'll see the value the next time someone hits a good return off your serve.

2. *React instantly.* Your brain has basically two ways of telling your body that it had better get itself up to the net for that drop shot, pronto. It *anticipates* what and where your opponent is going to hit, and it *reacts* to the ball once it has been hit.

React instantly and automatically to every ball your opponent hits.

Anticipation can only be improved with playing experience. I wish I could, but I can't teach it to you in this book. However, if you make a habit of reacting automatically to every ball your opponent hits, whether you think it's going in or not, your reactions will become reflexive, and you'll get to most balls whether or not you can anticipate. Watch the ball from a good ready position, see where it's going, react to that situation; then if the ball goes out or into the net, or if it's too good a shot, just cool it. Reacting only takes a fraction of a second; you can always cut it off if the ball goes out by just standing straight up out of your position. But it might have gone in, while you were deciding whether or not to move, hesitating because you didn't think it was worth making the effort for a ball that was probably going out. How many times have you stood flat-footed on that baseline, sure the ball was going to be long, and then watched it land right on the line and kick out of your reach? Makes you mad as hell, doesn't it? Makes me mad, too. *React to every shot your opponent hits without hesitation and don't rise up out of position until the point is absolutely over.*

3. *Get there quickly.*   "ONE-TWO! QUICK FEET!" A lady who took my clinic quoted me on her racket cover, so now I'll quote her back.

4. *Stop and set up as early as possible before you hit.*   There are two times during a point that you should strive to be stationary: when your opponent is hitting, and when you're hitting.

When you're having an easy rally, you and your friend just hitting to each other, for instance, you probably have no trouble setting up and hitting the ball, but when you have to run for it, do you usually end up running right through your shot instead of being there ready and waiting? It wouldn't surprise me if you had a good case of laziness and bad timing. Generally, average players run just hard enough to get to their shots and hit them on the run. For example, your opponent hits you a little dink lob. You lope back to it slowly, and before you know it the ball is descending behind you. What you should have done instead

(*Left*) Get there quickly: ONE-TWO! (*Right*) Set up for your shot as early as possible.

was hustle, set up, and be there waiting for the ball, in other words, *retimed* it—coordinated your timing with the ball's timing —and attacked it when you were in perfect position to hit the best shot you know how to make.

Whatever your caliber of tennis, you probably make your best shots when the ball is hit right to you. Because you are stationary, you have plenty of time to turn, plant your feet, and come forward into your shot. It's not easy, though, to find an opponent worth playing who is generous enough or dumb enough to hit right to you. But if you can be stationary—ready and waiting for the ball before it gets there—it's *as if* the ball had been hit right to you in the first place. You take your comfort range with you if you start out in good ready/playing position—with an aggressive, low profile—get a quick start, get to where the ball is going, and set up properly as early as possible.

5. *Recover immediately after every shot.* If you always assume that your opponent is going to return the ball until the point is

If you cross your feet up as you shuffle, you're going nowhere.

absolutely over, you'll never get caught napping. Make your shot, recover low and forward, and then get back into the court by running or by shuffling—skipping sideways in recovery position —which is better if you don't have too far to go because it doesn't commit your balance. Keep squared away both horizontally and vertically; you don't want your head, shoulders, or hips tilted to one side or the other. Don't cross your feet up as you shuffle back, because if the ball is hit while your feet are crossed, you're stuck going nowhere. You should come across with a bounce off your toes, maintaining shoulder-width between your feet; short steps are quicker and more controlled than giant ones.

8 ⚾ Running Drills

These are application drills. On the first day of my two-day clinics, I teach the techniques—ready position, stride pattern, quick start, pivoting, recovery, and so on—and on the second day we apply them in simulated and actual court situations. All four of these drills develop mobility skills—reflexes, balance, speed, and agility —by forcing you to exceed the normal requirements of the game. In the Balance and Motion Triangle, for example, you have to make 360-degree turns at a full run, which you'll never have to do in tennis unless you're playing in a tornado. But it will teach you to change direction quickly and under control. The Harness Drill, which requires you to pull a dead weight while you run, will help you develop snap in your step. In the Hit-and-Run Drill, you have to react instantly to the ball, without any clues to help you anticipate it, and in the Reaction Drill, you have even less time. They'll both help you develop ultrasharp reflexes on the court.

A number of people who work on these drills have told me that when they're playing tennis, they often find themselves thinking, "This is what I should be doing, just like in the drills."

While you're gaining quickness and control, the running drills will also improve your physical conditioning. Just knowing *how* to move isn't much use if you're too wiped out to put what you know into practice. Whether you play a drop shot/lob game, or you're a serve-and-volleyer, or you're a base-court player, tennis makes you move hard and fast. In a long match, you might have to run as much as five miles, and in that kind of tennis, it's often the guy with the best endurance who wins. The stamina to resist fatigue is the result of conditioning, which improves your circulatory, respiratory, and muscular systems. In addition, good endurance enables you to recover more quickly when you do get tired. It's also a fact that well-conditioned people experience a smaller rise in body temperature when they exert themselves than out-of-shape people.

Anyone who works out, young or old, advanced player or club hacker, can have good endurance. I know players in their fifties and sixties who can play four to five hours of tennis a day because they stay ahead of the game by exercising and working out. Runners develop endurance by overdistancing—a 440 runner will run hundreds of repeat 660s throughout the year so that he'll have plenty of stamina for his event. The body builds up endurance when it is *overloaded,* which is one reason I recommend doing the workouts and running drills *after* you've played tennis. (The other is simply that you won't tire yourself out before you play.) Overloading doesn't mean running until you collapse; overexerting yourself to that extent isn't good for you or your game. You should go just until you've extended yourself a little farther than you think you'd like. If you exert yourself a bit beyond your normal demands, your body will rise to the level required of it, and you'll develop more stamina not only for tennis but for everything else you do, too.

A word of caution: the week-end athlete, the fellow who plays five sets after doing nothing more strenuous the past week than walking to the car, is the one who's likely to have a medical disaster on the court. If you're really serious about getting in shape, and you're starting from way back, have a complete physical examination before you begin, and then start slowly and increase gradually. Stop when you feel overexerted. Be honest with yourself, and recognize the difference between enough and too much. Besides the danger to your heart, overstraining your body causes lactic acid to collect in your muscles, which makes them weak, and that's when you're most likely to tear or pull one. Besides, if you're tired, you won't do the drills well, and there's no sense in just going through the motions.

But when you are working on these drills, try to give them all you've got. A small number of repetitions well done will do more for you than many sloppy ones. You'll be able to increase the number as you get stronger and your wind improves. Establish a base—your starting performance—and work on extending it, beating your own records.

Your aim is to use a greater percentage of your athletic ability on the court. There will be times when you'll have nothing but that to rely on, to make the kind of spectacular gets that even your fiercest rival applauds. But most of the time, being quicker and stronger and in better shape will mean that you won't have to work as hard when you play; you'll find you can accomplish more with less effort. The better your endurance, and the more skillfully you can move, the smaller your half of the court will seem to you, and the bigger your opponent's.

BALANCE AND MOTION TRIANGLE

Stan Smith once told me that if he could improve his balance, he could improve his whole game. He's not the only one; you can't move well on the tennis court without good balance. Tennis requires that you make quick directional changes; if you can't shift your weight quickly, you'll do a lot of careening around on the court, lunging at the ball, hitting off the wrong foot, and staggering backward as you hit. Many players have problems keeping their balance for more than just a few steps. I see it all the time— folks trying to turn, for instance, by taking huge, tall steps, and by the time they've shifted, the ball is gone and they've lost the point.

Developing your balance—by challenging it—is the main purpose of this drill. Practicing these radical directional changes at a full run will make it easier for you to keep your balance when you play, because you will never have to change direction this drastically in any tennis match. Good balance, like good position, produces good strokes. The idea is to be able to stabilize your body in all kinds of trouble, because when you're in any situation on the court that requires a quick shift of direction, the more your balance is out of control, the less range you will have.

This exercise is a takeoff on the barrel race that horses run in *gymkhanas*. You need three tennis balls and a court, and, if possible, a stopwatch and someone to clock you. Place one tennis ball on the center line about three feet from the net, and the other two at the points where the service line intersects with the singles lines. Holding onto your racket, you're going to start from the center of the baseline, run around all three balls as fast as you can, and then run back to the baseline.*

Begin with the ball in the deuce court. Run to it as fast as you can: get your weight forward and down, keep a toe lead, and remember your stride pattern. When you get to that ball, don't slow down. Run around it as quickly as possible, making a clockwise turn. *Slide* around it if you can by dropping your weight way down and bracing yourself by putting your inside hand, which is your right, on the ground and leaning on it as you turn, so you should be holding your racket in your left hand. Take the turn at full speed and make as small a circle around the ball as possible —a four-foot diameter is very good. If you took it easy, slowing down and making big, wide circles around the ball, you wouldn't be challenging your balance. Make it difficult enough to do yourself some good.

People have a tendency to straighten up and lengthen their strides coming out of the turn, so this is where you should really concentrate on your form. Stan Smith, among others, agrees with

---

* If you're doing the drill off the court, place the balls as follows and begin at point X:

Balance and Motion Triangle: (*Above*) Brace yourself on the turn with your inside hand. (*Below*) You should be almost prone so you can slide around the ball.

(*Above*) Take the turn at full speed. (*Below*) Stay low and pump with
your arms coming out of the turn.

me that taking large steps is a major cause of being off-balance when you have to change direction. Stay low, pump with your arms and legs, and drive forward hard—pretend someone's holding you back as in the Harness Drill—and don't rise up any taller than you'd be when you normally hit the ball. Staying low will help you regain your balance quickly when you play, allowing you to have better equilibrium when you make contact with the ball.

After turning around the first ball, run cross-court to the ball in the ad court. Switch racket hands from left to right as you're running so that you'll have your inside (left) hand free to lean and turn on as you're making the ad court turn. This turn should be counterclockwise, so that you're making a full circle around the ball. Do it the same way: drop your weight way down and really speed around that ball.

Then race to the ball at net (keeping your racket in your right hand), run around it counterclockwise as fast as you can, and race back to the baseline.

You might fall down on the turns at first, because you're working against centrifugal force and gravity. Practice it until you can do the drill without falling, and then try to cut down your time by shaving off tenths of a second. If you really want to get your time down, work on chopping it out of the turns. I've run a lot of people through this drill, and so far Roscoe Tanner holds the world record at 7.4 seconds on clay, which is supposed to be a slow surface. I remember the first time he did it, with no instructions; it took him 9.8 seconds. Then I simply told him to stay low; he knocked off one second right away. He worked on it, and worked on it, until finally he was semiprone going through the turns, about two feet off the ground, sliding around the balls with absolutely beautiful control. It was really something to see.

This is also a great conditioning drill. Run through it five times, resting a minute or so between each one, so that you're still breathing a little heavily but have recovered enough not to hurt yourself. Really move it. It'll make you good and tired, and if someone who doesn't know what you're doing sees you he'll probably think you've lost your mind, but so what.

I usually wind up my clinics with a huge Balance and Motion Triangle relay race. I divide the group into two teams and line them up behind the baseline, using both sides of the court. Each team uses one racket and hands it off like a baton. It's incredible the way a race brings out everyone's competitive urge. I remember one guy saying to me afterward, "I stood on that line thinking, 'What's a grown man like me doing these silly races for?' Then when it was my turn, man, I put everything I had into it. I really wanted to *win*." Well, if you compete the same way against yourself, trying to beat your best performance, you'll get the maximum benefit from this exercise.

Incredible the way a race brings out everyone's competitive spirit.

HARNESS DRILL B

The Quick-Start Harness Drill on page 50 is a good one, with minor alterations, to help you develop the power you need in your feet and legs to *keep* running hard once you've gotten started. It's also a great conditioner for your circulation and wind.

Put a towel around your waist and have your partner hold the ends behind you. Then run forward while your partner pulls back just hard enough so that you can pull him into a walk but not a run. The difference between this drill and the Quick-Start Harness Drill is that (1) you take longer, but still very quick, strides; and (2) instead of taking just fifteen short, quick steps, you run all the way from the fence up to the net (a distance of about sixty feet, if you're doing it off the court), and back to the fence again if you have the strength—it should be a very tiring drill if you do it correctly. Then switch places with your partner and let him be a plowhorse for a while.

Remember that when you're the runner, you have to drop down

Harness Drill—great for leg power and conditioning.

low, shift your weight forward, and really pump with your arms. Your feet are pulling and straining, and you're using all your strength and energy to try to pull your partner down. (I hope you don't succeed, but that's how hard you should be pulling.) If you're not moving at all, he's pulling back too hard; tell him to ease up a bit, so that he's letting himself be pulled into a walk.

Don't get caught flat-footed. If your weight isn't on your toes, your partner is going to pull you straight back on your behind. But if you're *too* far forward, your feet will be behind you and you'll fall down. Have enough forward lean to maintain your balance and still be thrusting and driving ahead. I've noticed that often women tend to run a little prancingly—tiptoeing—almost as though they're trying not to make any noise when they run. This drill can help them learn to really put it to the floor.

When you're providing the resistance, maintain a steady, even pressure. If you get pulled into a run, you have to pull back harder.

You'll get more leverage if you bend your knees, keep a very wide base, and "sit back."

You can do this drill backward, too. The two of you face each other and the towel goes around the runner's back. The runner doesn't have as much strength this way, since your leg doesn't extend very far backward, so the person pulling back shouldn't resist as hard. You won't generate as much power or be able to develop a real stride going backward, but doing the drill in reverse will help you move more quickly when you have to run backward to chase a lob or hit an overhead.

REACTION DRILL

This is a very simple drill that can help you sharpen up your reflexes and decrease the time between when the ball is hit and when you react to it. Several people who do it have told me that it's improved their ability to stay with it when the action gets hot at net.

You don't need a court for this one. Stand in ready position, racket in hand. Your partner, who faces you, holds one ball in each hand and puts his hands behind his back. He takes one hand or the other, whichever pleases him, and thrusts it out in front of him as quickly as possible. As soon as you can tell which hand is coming, shift your body weight quickly to that side as though you're getting ready to hit a forehand or a backhand, and then get right back in ready position again. Your partner should try to test your anticipation, so he might hold out the same hand five times in a row. Similarly, when you're the one holding the balls behind your back, try to fool your partner. Alternate sides, or go to the same side, but be unpredictable. Make your partner work strictly on reaction, so that on the court you will both become like a couple of panthers.

HIT-AND-RUN DRILL

This drill will use and test just about everything you can learn from this book—agility, alertness, recovery, stride pattern, pivots,

The Hit-and-Run Drill tests just about everything you can learn from this book.

reflexes, balance. It will show you what your strengths are, and
what you need to work on. It requires two people and all those old
balls you've been saving to practice your serve. One person, the
thrower, stands near the net with the bucket of balls. The other,
the player, starts out in ready position on the baseline on the other
side of the net. The player needs his racket; the thrower does not.

First the thrower brings the player in by throwing him an easy
drop shot halfway between the service line and the net. The
player drops, pivots, runs in for it as quickly as he can, hits, and
recovers immediately. Meanwhile, the thrower throws the next
ball *as* the player is hitting the first one. If the player isn't recovering quickly enough, he won't be able to get to it.

The balls don't have to be thrown far and wide on the court
for this drill to be effective; you can work entirely within an eight-
or ten-foot range and still move the player around plenty. The
emphasis in this drill is on good form, not on where the ball goes
or just getting to it any old way. People will miss a bunch of balls
and think they're really messing up, but they're not, as long as
they're *getting* to the balls properly—maintaining their stride patterns, toe leads, correct arm-and-leg leads, and quick recoveries.
Don't worry about your stroking ability; it will come right back
when you're playing, along with new confidence in your capacity
to move on the court.

One of the main purposes of this drill is to develop inner-ball
quickness, so at least at first, work on close balls, within ten feet
or so of each other: a few to one side, a few to the other, mixing
them up. The player never really knows what's going to happen
in this drill, which is the beauty of it; he can't rely on his anticipation. You're trying to outguess each other just as in a tennis match,
but as the thrower you have all the control because you can always
fake, or do unexpected things, like throw eight straight balls to
the same side, or occasionally throw a wide one out if you're working on inner balls. People expect maybe two or three balls to the
same side, so if you drill away at that one side, the player will
learn that he can't throw his balance the other way in anticipation
because he won't be able to recover in time. He'll learn to recover

properly and be ready to go either way. Similarly, if he's playing too tall, he's going to have problems controlling these inner balls.

One of the most important things the player can learn from working on inner balls is to stay coiled—keyed up. You can be up at net in a position that *looks* aggressive, but just be posing, standing pat, not ready to unleash in either direction. When you're playing net and you hit a volley that's going to be easily returned, you've got to be ultraready because your opponent has the option of going across court, down the line, or lobbing over you. Whether you'll be ready for him or not is completely up to your reactions. In an aggressive game, you simply can't waste any time between when the ball is hit and when you're gone. Most of the action in this drill should take place inside the service line, where you have half the time to prepare that you would have on the baseline. Concentrate on coming into the ball with good cross-over footwork at net, and good recovery after you hit. Keep your weight down and in front and equally distributed on both feet.

It's throw-hit, throw-hit, side to side, up and back. Moving up and back gives many people more trouble than running from side to side, so be sure to work on it. As the thrower, feel the player out, and gear your throws to how well he's doing. Don't throw so slowly that he gets everything, or so fast that he can't get to anything, which would be frustrating and counterproductive. If the player doesn't have a chance to finish his shot before he recovers to get to the next ball, slow the pace down—let him finish his shot and throw immediately afterward. If he's really doing well, throw the ball a little sooner, or harder. But if anything, better too slow than too fast, because it's good form that's important. There's plenty of margin between difficult and impossible. When you're throwing wider balls, throw them a little more slowly so that the player can get to them. On wide balls, again, the most important thing is the recovery: the player has got to get ready to go for the next one. If he's hitting the ball and immediately running across to the other side, throw one behind him to make your point. The idea is to work on controlling every ball, being there in good position.

When I do this drill with someone for the first time, I begin by getting an idea of what the player can do. Say I'm working with a man or woman in his or her late fifties. I'll toss one out, see how the player works with it, then toss one out the other way and see how he works with that one. If he has problems reaching it, I throw the next one a little closer. If no problems, a little farther out. There'll be some balls that he can't get to; I use those as a guide. If a ball is out of his range, I shorten up a little bit, or give him more time, throwing it the same distance away but a little more slowly, because confidence is built with success. Take a ball someone can't reach and throw it just as wide but a hair more slowly. He gets to it, and he feels that he's done a great thing, which he has: broken through a barrier, discovered that a ball way the hell over there isn't unreachable after all. Then he finds himself really trying to get that outer ball, because he's seen that he can do it—and he's extended his range a little bit.

If I'm working, say, with a twelve-year-old junior, I'll draw him up first with a drop shot, making sure he has the correct leads, low posture, stride pattern, and so forth. That first ball should be easy enough for him to get to in plenty of time—not a "gimme" drop shot, but not so hard he feels he's lost right at the beginning. Then I might throw two or three easy outer balls to give him some pivoting practice, and then I'll bring him in to the center of the court with a ball near the center line and work him in there, because probably after a couple of long balls he's begun to get tired, and pretty soon he'll have had it. If I get him inside, I can give him another twelve or fifteen balls, so he'll get a good workout at the same time that he's working on his footwork, reactions, agility, balance, and so on. A junior in decent shape should be able to last about twenty balls.

If I'm working, say, with a forty-five-year-old overweight man, I'll start off with an easier drop shot, either back a little deeper or tossed up a little higher. For his wide ball, I won't throw as wide as for the kid. I may cut him off after eight or nine balls with a lob, because he'll probably be very tired by then.

It's a tiring drill. A man in one of my clinics once said it seemed as though it was never going to end. Don't let yourself get too fatigued, because when you're tired you probably won't move properly. Go until you're winded, take a rest, then do it again, or switch places with the thrower.

Try to build up your endurance. If you can go nineteen balls, aim for twenty-one. If you can go eight, try for ten, then twelve. Thirty balls thrown quickly and with some pace will get anyone tired. Build up from where you start—don't expect to go from eight to twenty in two days.

Clear the balls off the court periodically so that the player doesn't trip over them. And thrower—be alert so that you don't get hit by one, since you have no racket to shield yourself with.

Like the others, this drill can be done off-court if you don't have access to one for drilling. If the thrower stands about forty-five feet from the player, that will approximate the distance from the baseline to the other side of the net.

9 ⊕ Workouts

It's five games all, third set, two out of three. You've been going like gangbusters, racing in for drop shots, running down lobs, chasing cross-court shots. You want to win this match so badly you can taste it. Finally, you've got a chance to show your opponent once and for all who's boss. But at this point, you have a big problem. Your brain is yelling, "Come on, go after it! Get over there! Move!" but your body is whining, "I can't. I'd like to but I just can't move anymore. Everything is killing me. When is this going to be over? Let's default." You try squatting down between points to ease the pain in your legs, but standing up again takes too much effort, so you ditch that idea. You don't know how your legs, back, and head are going to get through this. Your side of the court, the side you've got to cover, looks like a big green lake. You let a drop shot go, mumbling "Nice shot" from the baseline. Your opponent is feeling and playing better every minute. Finally the set ends, 7–5 his, and you've lost the match.

Fatigue can be psychological. If you expect to be tired by the third set, or the fifth set, you probably will be. *Tired* can also be another word for *discouraged*. While it's true that everyone has an occasional energy crisis on the court, if you find yourself *always* getting tired when you play tennis, always having to face a whole set ahead of you that you don't want to play, you're probably out of shape. The only way you're going to solve that problem is to get *in* shape.

In the old days, before cars, TV sets, and supermarkets, people were generally stronger and in better condition. With the more relaxed life most of us lead now, hardly anyone is in good shape anymore, weekend tennis players included. Two or three hours of tennis each week just won't keep you in good enough shape to play your best if you're sitting behind a desk or a wheel the rest of the time. For one thing, to operate at maximum efficiency, you need more strength and endurance than a particular activity requires, so you'll never reach your full potential as a tennis player if you only play tennis. For another thing, in such a demanding sport, you're only as strong as your weakest area. If you haven't got good wind, that'll probably get you before anything else. Your back and stomach muscles, which are the ones that are most neglected in everyday life, are usually the muscles that wipe out first in a long match. Your legs go next, because they're doing most of the work. Once muscle fatigue starts to set in, you've got two opponents: the guy on the other side of the net and your own body. Recently I played with a friend who is just beginning to put some of my techniques into practice, but isn't in the kind of shape that would allow him to keep it up. I noticed that he did things more or less by the book for the first set, but then he began to tire and his game showed it. Balls he had surprised himself by getting to earlier he wasn't reaching anymore, and sometimes he wasn't even trying for them. He began waiting to see if my shot was going out instead of getting ready in case it went in; he started running through his shots instead of getting there early; he started playing too tall, and so on. When we came off the court, he told me that he now realized that what are usually thought of as bad habits are actually often caused by fatigue.

Good stamina is the result of an efficient cardiovascular system, an efficient respiratory system, and strong muscles. They all can be improved with training. The best way to build up your circulation and wind is with *aerobic* exercises, like the running drills in Chapter 8, which increase your capacity to utilize oxygen. The way to build up strength is by doing the workouts in this chapter.

The better your conditioning, the more you'll be able to do with less effort. The less you have to work against yourself, the better you'll play. You're also less likely to strain something if you're in shape, because when you've got tight, sore, used-up muscles, you're more injury prone. And if you do happen to injure yourself, good muscle tone helps you heal faster.

Most professional athletes use no more than fifty percent of their physical capacity when they compete. Obviously, average people playing tennis use a lot less. Now, if you just want to play what a friend of mine calls Hit and Giggle, you don't need any of this. But if you want to play more athletic, more aggressive tennis, which means playing with a lower and more forward profile, you're going to put more demands on your stomach, back, and leg muscles; staying on your toes throughout a whole match will be impossible if you're weak. Being in good condition will do as much for your tennis game as a new backhand, because improving your game is not only a matter of learning the proper techniques but also of being physically capable of carrying them out. All those lessons you've taken, all that practicing you've done, and all those tennis books you've read are pretty useless if you're too tired to execute what you've learned from them.

Being in good shape will also make you more confident on the court. If you know you can last as long as you have to, that your muscles, heart, lungs, joints, nervous system, and mind will be able to function at peak efficiency for a sustained period of time, that's a lot less to worry about. This is true no matter what level of tennis you play: beginning, intermediate, or advanced.

Your level of tennis also has nothing to do with how well you'll do at these workouts; the current state of your muscles does. Even among the pros, I've noticed that the guys who aren't getting at least to the semis most of the time find themselves almost as out of shape as if they weren't playing tennis at all. After the first time we worked out, Roscoe Tanner told me that every muscle in his body hurt, including the balls of his feet. He had to take a bath instead of a shower, because he could barely stand up. The second day of my clinic usually begins with a chorus of loud groans because of sore muscles from the first day. I remember once having an actor in my clinic who now spends more time playing in pro-celebrity tournaments than he does acting. Figuring that he was in great shape, he went all out on the workouts the first day. The second day he mostly spent holding up the wall. On the other hand, I've taught plenty of people who have found these exercises no strain at all, including one woman who could barely hit a tennis ball but goes to a gym every day. If you're just beginning to get in shape after a long period of not doing much exercise, start slowly and don't expect too much from yourself. If you're over age forty, or have any heart or other medical problems, check with your doctor first. Show him the book if you're not sure what you ought and ought not to do. If you have back problems, do everything slowly, especially the isotonic resistance exercises. That way you won't get caught in any strange positions you can't get out of.

These exercises are designed to be done with someone else, for several reasons. For one thing, people tend to work harder in pairs. It's also more fun to work out with someone else—you encourage each other, maybe compete a little—so you're more likely to keep it up. But most important, when you work out with someone else, you can better isolate the particular area you're working on: your partner serves as a weight with a brain, adjusting his resistance according to your strength; as you get stronger, he asserts more pressure. So work out with your doubles partner, or your opponent —you'll give each other a better game—or your husband or wife. I've also provided instructions for doing the exercises alone, so not having someone to work out with is no excuse! You also don't need a court for the workouts, so you can easily do them on days you're not playing tennis. I know one couple who does these exercises once or twice a week at home before dinner. When the husband took my clinic, he was about forty pounds overweight. No longer. He started working out, lost a few pounds at a time, then just decided the hell with being fat. He wound up losing thirty-odd pounds, just because he got excited about his body, working out, playing a lot of tennis, for the first time in ten or fifteen years. Before long his wife got the spirit, too. She's just a beginner in tennis, but they're both in terrific shape.

If you work out after playing, you're already warmed up, but if you're starting out cold, do the warm-ups first. I wouldn't recommend working out before playing because that would leave you too fatigued to play your best.

.Don't be too easy on yourself, or too hard. Go at your own pace, increasing the number of repetitions and the resistance as you progress. Compete with yourself, not with your partner. I've provided numbers; use them as a guide, but don't be rigid about it; you shouldn't exhaust yourself just to conform to my numbers. Remember that the quality of the work you do is just as important as the quantity. Women may want to do more repetitions with lighter resistance, which is the way to build strength without adding bulk.

ISOTONIC RESISTANCE DRILL, OR LEG LIFTS

Put on some shorts. Sit down with your legs out in front of you and take a look at them. Are they flabby and gooey or hard and solid? Have any waffles on your thighs? Well, if you do, I have a set of drills for you. They're called isotonic exercises, which simply means exercise in which the muscle contracts and moves against a load. They're great because they get the front, sides, and backs of your legs, and will help you develop the explosive power you need for quick starts. Go through the entire first section four times on your right leg, then four times on your left. Then do the next two sections the same way. When you've completed the entire drill, switch places with your partner. Use a towel or a mat if you're working out on a hard surface.

1. *For front of leg.* Lie flat on your back, legs straight, feet together, arms at your sides. Your partner, kneeling by your right leg, grasps your right ankle with his right hand and places his left

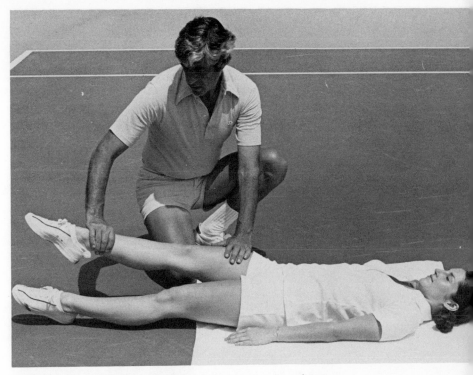

Raise your leg as high as possible against partner's resistance.

hand on your right thigh. Raise your leg straight up as high as possible while your partner applies pressure against it, resisting your movement so that you really have to work to lift it up. It should take twelve full counts (one count per second) to get your leg up as high as it will comfortably go. Try to maintain a rhythm; the rise should be evenly distributed across the twelve counts.

Obviously, each person's strength differs. If you're trying hard and are nonetheless unable to budge your leg, your partner is exerting too much resistance and should ease up a bit. Also, watch out for cramps, a sign that your partner is applying too much pressure. Before cramps occur, you leg will begin to quiver a little. If this happens, rest a minute before continuing.

Your partner now stands, holding your leg up by the ankle while you relax it completely. He then walks around to a position just above your head and pulls your leg back very slowly and carefully toward him, stretching it gently without straining or

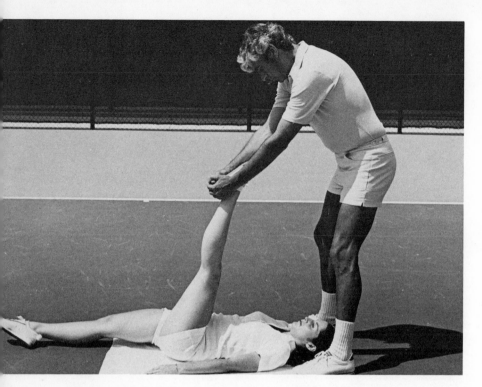

Partner pulls your leg very slowly and carefully toward him.

bouncing it, because bouncing it would stretch the muscle too fast. Let him know when to stop. This is a valuable stretch, but don't overdo it. You want to get looser but you can't do the whole job in one day.

Your partner now returns to your right side, still holding your relaxed leg up, and bends it fully at the knee until your heel is almost touching the back of your upper thigh. He then puts both hands on your knee and pushes it back gently toward your chin to stretch your hips and back a bit. Remember to communicate so that you don't overdo these stretches.

Next, keeping his right hand on your knee, your partner pins down your right shoulder with his left hand and pushes your knee over to the left, toward your left armpit. This should be done especially slowly and carefully.

Next he brings your bent leg back across to the right, and lifts it straight up again, both hands grasping your ankle. Now he

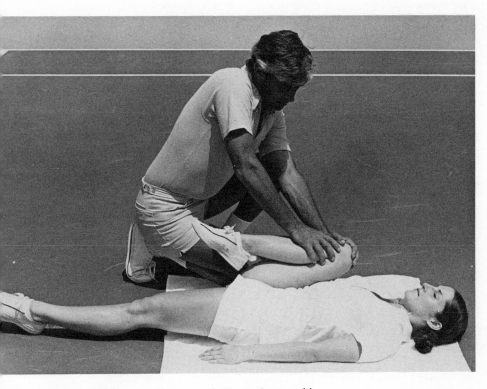

Partner pushes your knee gently toward your chin.

Partner pushes your knee slowly and carefully toward your armpit.

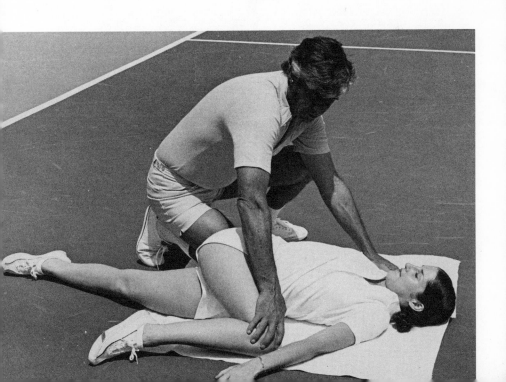

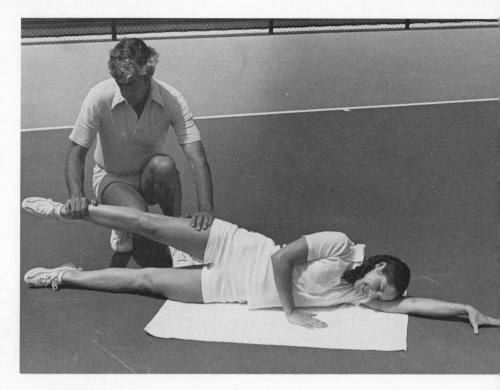

Lying on your side, raise your leg while partner exerts pressure downward.

exerts resistance as you lower your leg to the floor with all your strength for a full twelve counts.

Do each movement four times for each leg, not alternating legs. Work up to seven or eight times for each leg, and increase the count to fifteen, seventeen, twenty seconds, your partner exerting more pressure as you progress.

2. *For sides of legs.* Lie on your left side, legs straight, left arm cushioning your head, right arm braced in front of you for balance. Your partner, kneeling by your legs, grasps your right ankle with his left hand and places his right hand on your thigh. Raise your leg against his resistance for a full count of twelve. Keep your leg straight; many people tend to bend it, which would make the exercise easier. When you've raised your leg as high as it will go, your partner grasps your ankle with both hands and

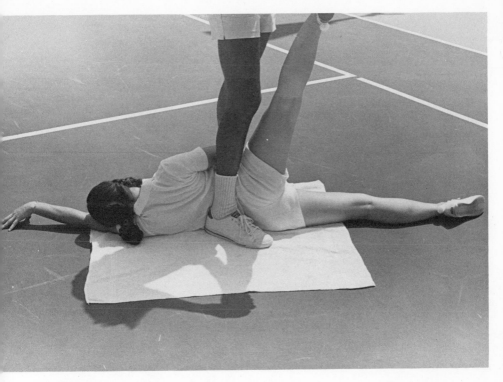

Partner puts his foot in the small of your back to keep your hip socket "locked."

stands straddling your body. Relax your leg for several seconds. Your partner then stretches it back gently a little farther, without straining it. To keep your hip socket "locked" as he stretches your leg back in this side position, your partner should put his right foot directly in the small of your back, pulling your leg straight along the line of your body. Once the leg is stretched back, relax it for several seconds.

Then, from this point of maximum stretch, begin to lower your leg for a count of twelve, your partner straddling your body and "walking" your leg down as he resists your pull. This will strengthen your inner thigh and groin area, where so many people are weak, and replace the fat with muscle. After working on your right leg four times, turn over onto your right side and repeat on your left leg four times. Again, work up to seven or eight repetitions, and increase the count and the resistance.

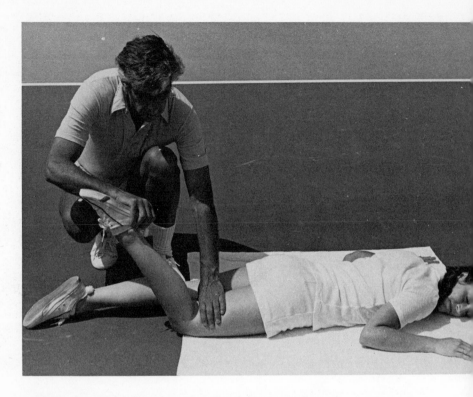

Raise the lower half of your leg against partner's resistance.

3. *For backs of legs.* Lie on your stomach, legs straight, arms at sides. Your partner, kneeling, grasps your right ankle with his right hand and places his left hand on the back of your knee. Bending it at the knee, raise the lower half of your leg against his resistance for twelve counts.

Now relax your leg as your partner pushes your heel in as close to your rear end as possible to stretch and loosen your quadriceps muscle. When he has pushed your leg in as far as it will go, push back against his resistance for twelve counts, finishing with your leg straight. Do four for each leg.

You may be a little wobbly-legged after these isotonics at first; better now than during the third set. I've heard from many people that since they've been doing them regularly, they have no problems staying on their toes throughout a match. To do them alone, make it an isometric drill by putting your feet under a heavy couch

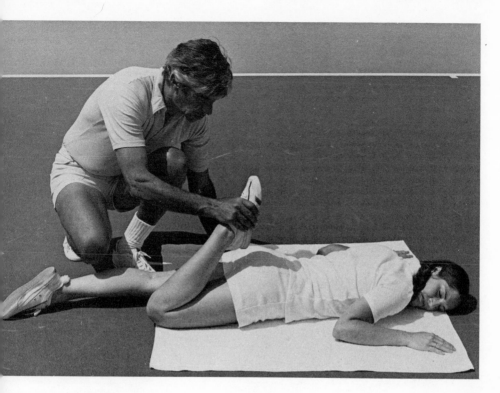

Partner pushes your heel toward your rear end.

and pushing up against it for twelve counts in all three positions. The only part you won't be able to duplicate is the stretches.

SADDLE DRILL

I used to call this the Obscene Drill because it looks, well, strange, but it's a terrific exercise for isolating and strengthening your calf muscles. This drill won't build up bulk; it'll just make your calves stronger and more limber, which will help you run a lot more quickly on the court.

With your feet slightly more than shoulder-width apart, stand facing a solid wall, about three feet away from it. Lean forward and place both hands against the wall at about head height, as though you're about to be frisked. Keeping your hands on the wall, move back a few steps so that your rear end sticks out. Point

The Saddle Drill is terrific for your calf muscles.

your toes in slightly. Your partner either hops or mounts from a chair onto the small of your back, just above your rear end, and holds onto your shoulders as you do toe raises, lifting up on your toes as high as you can, then lowering without touching your heels to the ground. Keep your knees and back straight. Work up from one set to three sets of twenty, alternating between sets with your partner.

Although this drill does not put very much stress on your back, if you have back problems, check with your doctor before you do it. I once had a woman in my clinic who weighed 106 pounds, whose partner was a 250-pound man. Her husband was absolutely horrified when he saw that huge man get on his wife's back. She was pretty scared too, but carrying him turned out to be no problem at all for her. However, just to be on the safe side, I recommend trying it first with someone much lighter than yourself, or just have someone bear down on your shoulders with his hands. If you're working out alone, you can do this drill with a weight belt, or a backpack, or, if you're tall enough, by pressing up with your hands against the top of a doorway instead of against a wall.

KICK-UPS

Have you ever played a couple of sets and found your serve getting weaker and weaker each time you served, until you had a better chance of winning on your opponent's serve than on your own? You might be losing your serve because your stomach and back muscles are weak. Since they're rarely used, they're usually only slightly developed. Kick-ups are much better for these muscles than sit-ups, as you'll see the morning after you first do them. This exercise is best done with a partner of similar size and strength. If you're using a towel, fold it in quarters and place it under the small of your back, so that you don't take off any skin.

Lie flat on your back, feet together, toes pointed. Your partner straddles you, facing your feet, his feet near your armpits. Grasp his ankles, raise both your legs, and let your partner catch them. Your partner throws your legs down hard first to the left, then

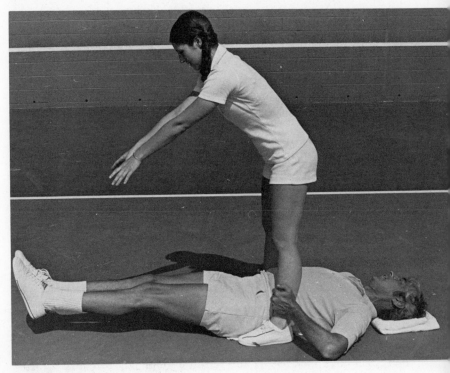

Kick-Ups: Don't let your heels touch the ground between kicks.

to the middle, then to the right, middle, left, and so on, and each time you kick them back up as forcefully as you can. Don't let your heels touch the ground between each kick. Keep your knees locked and your head on the ground. Begin with two sets of twenty, alternating with your partner between sets, and work up gradually to three sets of one hundred.

FIGURE EIGHTS

This one hits almost every muscle in your back, stomach, and legs. In 1974, I worked out with the U.S. Davis Cup Team in Palm Springs, shortly before they played Mexico. John Andrews was hurting so badly from these last two exercises that he was sure he had an ulcer. All he had was weak stomach muscles.

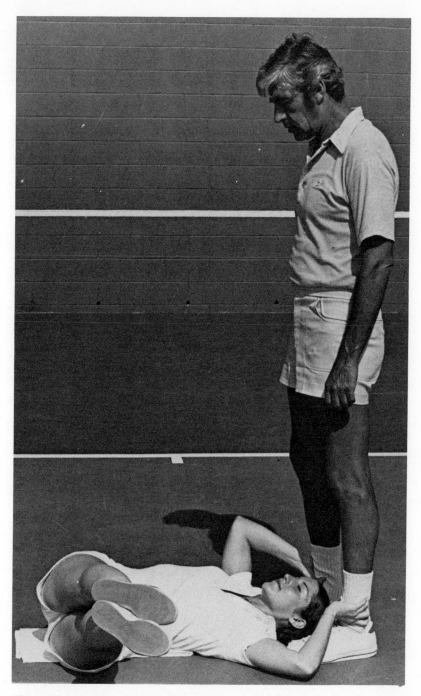

Figure Eights will really help tighten your stomach muscles.

Lie prone. Your partner stands straddling your head; you grasp his ankles for support. (Grasp the legs of a heavy chair if you're doing this one or kick-ups alone.) Raise your feet six inches or so off the ground and swing your whole trunk all the way around to the right, trying to get your feet way up, level with your shoulders. Then, without letting them hit the ground, swing your feet all the way back around to the left to shoulder-level, then back around to the right, and so on. This one is really hard, so start off with fifteen and try to work up to one hundred one of these fine days.

10 ⊗ How to Use This Book—
Some Guidelines

Let's face it: this is not a book you can just read once, put on the shelf, and presto—go out and play better tennis. While there are things in here that you can start doing right away, such as playing lower and more forward, you'll probably find that to maintain your good ready position for any length of time, you're going to need more strength than you now have. Most of the techniques and skills in this book—getting a correct stride pattern; getting a quick start; pivoting correctly; developing better balance, quickness, and agility—are going to require practice, strength, and endurance. This chapter will give you an idea of how much working out and practicing you should be doing according to your particular goals and the time you can devote to improving your game.

Charlie Pasarell notes that it's not how he feels the day of a tournament that determines how well he'll do, but rather what he's done the week and more before: if he's practiced hard, taken good care of himself, gotten in good shape, he's fairly assured of playing well that day, instead of having to leave it to chance and inspiration. You get stronger and in better shape through a process of breaking down and building up.

Overloading—putting more stress on your body than it's accustomed to—breaks your body down. It's what's happening when you can't run any farther, lift any more weight, or chop any more wood because you feel tired and sore. If you were to go out and play three hard sets right now, you'd probably exhaust yourself. But if you kept it up, playing regularly and getting enough rest and proper nutrition, you would build up tissue and become stronger. Those three sets would gradually become easier and easier, until six months from now, you could handle them with no problem. Your body would have risen to accommodate the stress you were putting on it without having to strain. But you wouldn't have just gotten steadily stronger and in better shape. Each time you pushed yourself past your current capacity, you would have overloaded—broken down—and then built up a little further.

Obviously, if you can get yourself in shape early in the season, you're going to be that much ahead of the game. In fact, a number of the pros are talking about doing just that: getting together every January before the new season, probably in Puerto Rico, to work out and train. Other sports have training camps; why not tennis?

Before you run out to practice your pivots and run Balance and Motion Triangles, a few words for the would-be fanatic: take it easy. Building up has to be a gradual process. There are athletes who are weakened by overtraining—they work out every single day, constantly breaking down, never giving their bodies a chance to rebuild. Remember that you have to do the workouts and drills in this book in conjunction with rest, which in some cases might simply mean more mild exercise, depending on where you're starting from. Have a hard workout one day, play a few sets the next day—fine, though you're probably not going to get much out of your body that next day.

Also, remember that even the pros have days when they get out on the court and can't do anything right, especially when they're working on something new that throws off the rest of their game. They try not to let it bother them because they know it's only temporary; probably the next day they'll be right back in the groove. So don't be discouraged or give up on a new skill or technique if you don't get immediate results.

The schedule below is for people who are very serious about their games: a guy or gal who plays on a high school, college, or local team; a young junior who wants to make the team or enter tournaments; someone who would like to turn pro; anyone in a competitive situation where he or she is playing tournaments weekly or monthly. If you're a junior, or have any questions, you might want to show this book to your coach or local pro so that he or she can help you get started correctly.

Monday: Work out hard. Do everything in this book—the warm-ups, the pivots and the rest of the footwork, and all the drills and workouts, which are the things that build strength and stamina. To go through the whole program should take you between two and a half and three hours.

Tuesday: Play a lot of tennis; work on form and strokes. You're recuperating from Monday's workout today, not trying to extend yourself any farther.

Wednesday: Play in the morning, work out in the afternoon. You want to break down again today by working out on top of practice.

Thursday: Practice; do a lot of hitting. You're resting a bit from Wednesday and working on your game at the same time.

Friday: Catch up by resting. You may want to go out and jog a little, stretch a bit—just light work so you don't break down again.

Saturday and Sunday: Spend what you've earned.

Monday: Start all over again.

That's a heavy schedule, working out two days a week, playing three days a week. It's for people who are very ambitious and can make the time for it. Less active, less competitive players can do proportionately less. It's a very individualized matter. I know one woman, for instance, who works out about once a week most of the time, which keeps her in pretty good shape, but shifts to a heavy schedule like this for a month before she's playing in a tournament, which really sharpens her edges.

Let's say you're a woman who plays tennis every morning and you want to improve your game. You're not trying to be Chris

Evert; you'd just like to beat your tennis friends. If you have the time, you should try to work out once a week; you might want to play in the morning and drill in the afternoon. You'll probably be surprised at how much stronger, quicker, more efficient, and more confident you'll be on the court, and so will your tennis friends.

Say you're a club hacker who plays three or four nights a week if you're lucky. If you can make the time to work out—to do everything in this book—on a schedule of once a week, that will do you and your game a lot of good.

If you're a weekend athlete, those eight days a month that you have to play tennis are probably very precious to you, and you may not have the time to go through the whole program. If that's the case, the things to concentrate on are your stomach, your back, and your legs, which are probably your weakest areas. If it's raining some Saturday, or you have nothing else to do, get a partner and do the isotonic resistance exercises and some of the other workouts; you may want to do the running drills one Sunday after you play. Often, even if the weather isn't good enough for tennis—too cold or windy—you can still go out and get some exercise. You don't need a court for most of the things in this book; you can do them in a park, on a field, in a parking lot, wherever it's convenient for you. Working out a few minutes here, a few minutes there, or even once a week won't get you in top shape, but it will do you a lot of good, tightening your stomach and strengthening your legs a bit for the next weekend. You'll have more strength and energy and an ability to do things you weren't able to do before. Once you start seeing some results from training, you might even decide that you can make more time for it.

By the time my clinic ends, everyone on the court, including me, has had a real workout and is practically too exhausted to move. That's when I point out that just participating in the clinic for two days and not following it up by practicing what you've learned is like spending a weekend on a fat farm and then going back to spaghetti and ice cream sundaes at home. Reading this book is only the beginning. Since you're bound to benefit from whatever aspects of the program you apply, how much you get out of it is up to you. Good luck.